Sir,

Published by Times Books

An imprint of HarperCollins Publishers
Westerhill Road, Bishopbriggs
Glasgow G64 2QT

HarperCollins Publishers
Macken House, 39/40 Mayor Street Upper
Dublin 1, D01 C9W8, Ireland

First edition 2023

HarperCollins would like to thank all correspondents who have given permission for
their letters to appear in this volume. Every effort has been made to contact and credit
the copyright owners of material quoted in this book. If any omissions have been made
please contact us.

A catalogue record for this book is available from the British Library.

Thanks and acknowledgements go to Joanne Lovey and Robin Ashton at News
Licensing and, in particular, at The Times, Ian Brunskill and, at HarperCollins,
Harley Griffiths, Evangeline Sellers, Kevin Robbins and Rachel Weaver. With special
thanks to Judith Anthony.

ISBN 978-0-00-864339-3

10 9 8 7 6 5 4 3 2 1

Printed in the UK using 100% Renewable Electricity at CPI Group (UK) Ltd

If you would like to comment on any aspect of this book,
please contact us at the above address or online.
e-mail: times.books@harpercollins.co.uk

www.timesbooks.co.uk

I am sometimes asked to give my favourite "bottom-right". There are too many to mention, though two in particular come to mind. The first, from Paul Thomas, and published on April 16, 2015, is part of a correspondence on what to do with published (and, later, unpublished) letters to *The Times*: "Sir, My French daughter took photocopies of my letters, enlarged them to A4 size, stuck them together and dyed them pink — and now uses them as a sunshade in her lounge in Paris. When guests come to dinner they are asked to translate at least three letters into French, Russian and Chinese with the aid of dictionaries. The first to complete the task wins a bottle of Moët & Chandon and a slice of homemade dacquoise." For sheer oddity this one is hard to beat.

The second, from Richard Martin, on the subject of football chants, and published on July 2 the same year, could not be more different: "Sir, During the England v Germany women's friendly at Wembley last year, as the German goalkeeper was preparing to take a goal kick I began the chant that I had heard sung at every football match I had ever attended during the previous 43 years: 'Yooooooooooooooooou fat bastaaaaarddddddd ...' There was a sharp intake of breath from about 30,000 female spectators, who all turned to look at the source of this invective. My daughter leaned across and whispered, 'You must never - *ever* - call a woman fat ... Not even an opposition goalkeeper ... Not even if England women were in a penalty shootout at the end of a World Cup final.'"

I would like to thank Royston Robertson for his fine cartoons but most of all I would like to pay tribute to the loyal army of *Times* readers, without whose wit, erudition and eloquence this book would not have been possible. To you I say: keep on writing!

Andrew Riley Letters editor, *The Times*, London SE1

Introduction

The history of *The Times* is festooned with weighty letters from the great and the good, who since 1785 have regarded the paper as their first port of call when any affairs of state need addressing – something that King George V was quick to recognise when a friend asked him for some regal assistance: "My dear fellow, I can't help you. You'd better write to *The Times*."

Many of those letters have been lauded over the years, and rightly so. This slim volume, though, celebrates the quirky and the humorous, in other words the humble "bottom-right" letter. Some of them appeared elsewhere on the page because this highly coveted slot was already taken, but in spirit they are all "bottom-rights". *Times* readers, I have found, are without peer in their range of interests, expertise, experience, knowledge, eloquence and wit, as this book demonstrates.

Humorous letters have appeared in the paper since its earliest days, but the "bottom-right" as a national institution dates to the 1950s, when Geoffrey Woolley was Letters editor. This tradition continues, with the ideal letter to *The Times* once described in *The Spectator* as "an alchemy of proposition and declamation, a shooting star of reason, a dark vein of English eccentricity, a merciless slash of common sense". I have only one quibble with that definition: it seems to me, from the hundreds of thousands of letters submitted by *Times* readers that I've had the privilege of reading, that this fêted English eccentricity is in fact British.

Brevity remains the soul of wit, as Shakespeare noted, and this is certainly true of the "bottom-right". The opposite is also true: the most common reason for the rejection of a letter for publication is overwriting. This, however, does not seem to have prevented the publication of an 11,071-word letter on October 13, 1898. It was from Sir Godfrey Lushington, permanent undersecretary of state of the Home Office, on the now-forgotten Dreyfus affair, and is the longest letter that *The Times* has ever run. We will not see its like again.

Foreword

A newspaper is only as good as its readers, and *The Times* is fortunate to have intelligent, sophisticated and brilliantly funny ones, as the letters in this book testify. Witty writing takes time and imagination, and it is clear that correspondents to our newspaper have thought long and hard about both their subjects and their sentence structures.

This selection of highlights from the letters page of the past twelve months makes clear that *Times* readers are an erudite and unpredictable lot. Eager to debate the great issues of the day, from AI to the cost of living, they are no less frequently exercised by more recondite matters such as the correct address for in-laws, the Dijon mustard shortage and ancient Hoovers.

It is intimidating for a newspaper editor to receive a missive from a reader whose knowledge of a subject dwarfs that of the paper's own specialist reporters. And it is a distinct pleasure to receive a letter from a clever and amusing correspondent. We owe our readers a great debt.

Tony Gallagher Editor, *The Times*, London SE1

Contents

THE TIMES

Sir,

The year in letters

Edited by Andrew Riley

TIMES BOOKS

Arts, culture and sport

Casting conundrum

Sir,
If able-bodied actors may not play Richard III, as the outgoing head of the *Royal Shakespeare Company* has suggested (report, May 6), then surely neither may commoners, because they do not have the relevant "lived experience". Only a disabled member of the monarchy will do.

Roderick Shaw Edinburgh

Sir,
As an actor, I live in my imagination. That is my lived experience, as it was that of Shakespeare, Shaw and Sarah Kane ("Casting conundrum", letter, May 7). The theatre is a gymnasium of the imagination — both actors and audiences stretch their imaginations there. Remove that element and you have a mere moving photograph.

Simon Callow London N8

Fabulous failure

Sir,
Your mention of the wonderful line by Stephen Fry's husband, "I don't know what you're fussing about — we're not late yet", TMS, May 30, reminded me of my time as a curator at the Tate Gallery. A drawing that had been misplaced in the storeroom had been missing for weeks, and I asked the art handlers responsible whether it had been located. Sheepishly, one of them replied: "We've almost found it."

Paul Moorhouse London N10

Just Shakespeare

Sir,
Whenever the perennial argument questioning Shakespeare's authorship of the plays is raised, I think of another great English writer gently ridiculing the idea in "William holds the Stage", written in 1932 by Richmal Crompton. An old boy at William's school, Mr Welbecker, comes to lecture his class and seeks to persuade the boys that it was Bacon who wrote the plays. When asked to summarise Mr Welbecker's talk by his headmaster, William's confused explanation that someone called Ham or Eggs or Bacon wrote Shakespeare's work is joyous and consigns any academic debate to all that it can be: mere fancy and conjecture.

Keith Robinson Hoylake, Wirral

Word of truth

Sir,
Further to James Marriott's article "Eng Lit is doomed by loss of cultural prestige", Jun 30, Frank McCourt gave perhaps the most robust defence of English literature courses when asked by his students why they should read Chinua Achebe's *Things Fall Apart*. "You will read it for the same reasons why your parents waste their money on your piano lessons," he replied. "So you won't be a boring little shite the rest of your life."

Andrew Copeman Teacher of English, Latymer Upper School, London W6

Statues must stand

Sir,
Libby Purves ("Prim distaste for statues ignores our story", Jul 4) urges restraint over statue destruction. As it was she who successfully put me in the draw for the empty plinth in Trafalgar Square, I briefly became such a monument (in full Morris dance rig, playing a melodeon). As such I wholly support her sentiment.

Patrick Purves Louth, Lincs

Sir,
Libby Purves is on the money, other than her discussion of any hypothetical statue of the prime minister. Yes, a Boris Johnson statue in marble or granite would be most sculptors' "bad hair" day. But were it modelled in plaster and cast in bronze, the hairdo would be their dream, and the statue would "quiver with life". That phrase comes from Jacob Epstein; it is a shame that he is no longer with us to rise to the challenge.

Dr Mark Stocker, FSA Christchurch, New Zealand

Hot under the collar

Sir,
As a surviving cast member of *It Ain't Half Hot, Mum*, allow me to contradict Penny Mordaunt's claim that the show was guilty of "casual racism, homophobia, white privilege, colonialism, transphobia, bullying, misogyny and sexual harassment" ("How Mordaunt wound up the nostalgia lobby", David Aaronovitch, Jul 14). As witnessed by our co-author, Bombardier Jimmy Perry,

the British Army in India was indeed possessed of all those dubious attributes. All we did was to reflect them.

Stuart McGugan (aka Gunner "Atlas" Mackintosh, Royal Artillery Concert Party, Deolali, India)
West Bilney, Norfolk

Niche museums

Sir,
May I put in a word ("Our story through the wonder of small relics", Libby Purves, Jul 18) for the Pencil Museum in Keswick, which enlivened many a wet holiday in the Lakes. I can never understand why my children never take my grandchildren.

Tony Langley Chorley, Lancs

Sir,
I was keen to visit the Trolleybus Museum near Doncaster, which has the largest collection of such vehicles in the world. Sadly, its website says that it is "poorly served by public transport".

Dominic Regan Bath

Sir,
Further to the Trolleybus Museum in Sandtoft being poorly served by public transport (letter, Jul 21), the James Herriot Museum in Thirsk does not admit dogs.

Nicholas Binns Darley Dale, Derbyshire

Sir,
The Lawnmower Museum in Southport has a *Lawnmowers of the Rich and Famous* exhibition, with items previously owned by Princess Diana, Brian May, Vanessa Feltz and Richard and Judy. For those not interested in garden machinery, it also houses a key museum.

John Burscough Brigg, Lincs

Monster munch

Sir,
Your article about BBC sound effects ("Unsung stars of crashes and roars make it into spotlight", Jul 18) reminded me of my own contribution many years ago. Working on features and drama and recording a comedy show in which a wife phoned her husband to say there was an iguana in the cellar eating the coal, I was told to get a packet of crisps from the canteen, and at the relevant moment to eat them noisily in front of the microphone to simulate an iguana having its lunch.

Jennifer Alexander London

Sound of the pit

Sir,
The letter about BBC sound effects (Jul 21) reminds me of when as a stringer for the BBC I was asked to provide a report "with actuality" (background sound) on the closing of Chislet Colliery in Kent in 1969. I taped my piece in the pit's engine winding room, where the miners were brought up in cages after finishing their shifts.

On returning home I played the tape back, only to find that the sound did not register. Eventually I had a eureka moment: I recorded the piece again while rattling my wife's hairdryer in an old biscuit tin.

Malcolm Mitchell Barham, Kent

Brolly with wings

Sir,
On the subject of sound effects in radio (letters, Jul 21 & 26), when I was a studio manager in drama I was confronted with a request for the sound of a pterodactyl flying past. I achieved this by running while opening and shutting an umbrella.

Dame Esther Rantzen Bramshaw, Hants

Austen for all

Sir,
James Marriott's column ("Even Netflix stinker gets Jane Austen's genius", Jul 21) reminded me that as a young English teacher in the 1970s I was visited by a militantly modernist school inspector who was openly scornful that the class was reading *Pride and Prejudice*. She was quite put out to find that they were enthusiastic about the novel and asked rather sharply: "So why do you like it?" The response was immediate. Pointing to a classmate, one girl said, "Well you see, because Anne is exactly like Lydia", to general agreement, even from Anne herself. Which said it all, really.

Aline Templeton Tenterden, Kent

Neighbours addicts

Sir,

I much enjoyed reading about Sir Stephen Spender's secret obsession with *Neighbours* (Saturday Review, Jul 23). My father, Brian Johnston, shared this fixation and made sure he was not broadcasting on *Test Match Special* whenever an episode was being aired. He shared this secret love of the programme with his close friend Sir Paul Getty; it was not unusual for Sir Paul to phone Brian at home to discuss that day's revelations. My parents even travelled up to Stockport to take "Harold" and "Madge" out for dinner, when they were performing in panto there. When my father died in 1994 the BBC arranged a memorial service at Westminster Abbey and, despite the dean's reservations, the congregation departed to the theme music of *Neighbours* played by the band of the Grenadier Guards.

Andrew Johnston Wykey, Shropshire

Path to fame

Sir,

I was smiling at the wit of George Bernard Shaw (The last word, Aug 8), "Martyrdom . . . is the only way in which a man can become famous without ability," when it occurred to me that the great man evidently never foresaw the advent of *Love Island*.

Lynnette Cassidy Huddersfield

Banal buys

Sir,
Further to Carol Midgley's Notebook (Aug 20) on reviews of mundane purchases, further hours of entertainment can be derived from the ability on Amazon to see all the reviews posted by a particular user. A fellow author once used this facility upon being given a particularly snarky review for one of her works. She shared a screenshot of both the book review (one star) and a review for haemorrhoid cream (also one star) posted by the same reviewer, with the tagline: "Blimey, I never thought the curse would actually work."

Fiona Valpy Dunkeld, Perthshire

It's just not cricket

Sir,
Regarding Matthew Syed's piece on the "Mankad" rule ("I'm guilty of 'pulling a Mankad' – but please let me explain myself", sport, Sep 28), on one occasion when I was captain of my cricket team I advised my bowler, in a very loud voice so that there was no confusion over what I was saying, that he had my permission to run out the non-strike batsman the next time he stole a yard or so before the ball had been delivered. It did the trick, though conversation over drinks in the pub later was less jolly than usual.

Michael Turner Hull

Dangerous wit

Sir,

Two of Alan Rickman's well-known witty ripostes are mentioned in yesterday's TMS (Oct 5). However, I was told by Lindsay Duncan that when they were co-starring in *Les Liaisons Dangereuses* she was amused when he whispered in her ear, before going on: "Just to warn you, tonight I am flirting with inaudibility." I think I was at that performance.

Sir Michael Codron Aldwych Theatre, London WC2

Drama queen

Sir,

Richard Morrison (Saturday Review, Oct 15) wonders what Queen Mary might have made of the Queen Mother's remark to two gay footmen: "Would one of you old queens mind getting this old queen a drink?" She may not have been as shocked as Morrison thinks: when the honours list was presented to her, it was her habit to consult her friend, the actor Ernest Thesiger, as they sat embroidering together, on the sexual persuasion of nominees. "Mr Gielgud?" the Queen would ask. "As a coot, ma'am," would come the reply, as the actor's sharp needle pierced the fabric, "as a coot."

Simon Callow London N8

Artist on a roll

Sir,

Matthew Parris's reference to Izal lavatory paper (Notebook, Nov 2) evoked memories of my 1950s boyhood drawing on strips torn from this antiseptic-smelling paper: a cheap alternative to a sketchbook. Similarly, Stanley Spencer made preparatory sketches for his wartime *Shipbuilding on the Clyde* paintings on lengthy rolls of lavatory paper.

Peter Saunders Salisbury

Nose for quality

Sir,
Katy Perry and your leading article both omit to mention the unique smell of newspapers and the paper on which they are printed ("Perry sings praises of reading the paper", Nov 4). They all differ but *The Times* is quite recognisable — it always adds to my enjoyment of reading the paper.

Anthony Stanbury Southrop, Glos

Emphatic mark

Sir,
The slammer, the screamer, the bang, the gasper and the shriek are all terms for the much-berated exclamation mark (Feedback, Nov 5). Perhaps innate gentility prohibited mention of the most common expression used by typesetters in the days of the printing press: "a dog's cock". I remember frequently being tickled by this expression as a young lad, listening to my father, who was a reporter, phoning his copy over to the news desk of the Newcastle Journal.

Geoff Brownlee Hornby, N Yorks

Eating fish in a lift

Sir,
I was fascinated by the "smelly fish in the lift" argument ("Insisting on free speech 'is like eating fish in a lift'", Nov 7). I wonder what Andrew Boggs might have made of the young woman in the front row of the Coliseum for a performance of *Tosca* last week who not only removed her shoes and stuck her feet on the rail in front of her but then proceeded to munch away on a very oniony-smelling wrap a few feet away from the wonderful singers giving their all for her entertainment on the stage.

Suzie Marwood London SW6

Theatre is no picnic

Sir,
I cannot agree more with Suzie Marwood ("Eating fish in a lift", letter, Nov 9). Surely it is time to call an end to eating after curtain-up. Nobody should arrive at the theatre so hungry that they desperately need an onion wrap or, as was the case during the second half of *King Lear* at the Globe recently, a family-sized bag of tortilla chips. We should pull the plug on picnicking during a performance.

David Isaac London N2

A cast too far

Sir,
Your all-encompassing obituary of David English (Nov 14) contains the wonderful line that he made

"an appearance alongside Laurence Olivier, Sean Connery, Robert Redford and Michael Caine in Richard Attenborough's 1977 epic war film *A Bridge Too Far*." I too was an extra in that film, as an unseen crewman in a Sherman tank crossing the bridge at Nijmegen. I shall adopt the same line from now on.

Malcolm Watson Ryde, Isle of Wight

Misheard lyrics

Sir,
Concerning misheard lyrics ("Springsteen admits 50-year blunder on Thunder Road lyric", Nov 16), some years ago I pointed out to Sir Tim Rice that the title of his composition *High, Flying, Adored* from *Evita* had appeared on the sleeve of a new recording as *High Flying Doors*. His response was that I had obviously not heard his moving tribute to aircraft exits.

Keith Turner Horringer, Suffolk

Handle on Handel

Sir,
Michael Mannix asks if he is alone (letter, Nov 23) in regarding the *Messiah* as one of Handel's dullest works. I think he probably is. Why would such a "dull" composition be recorded nearly 250 times and have attracted the attention of Mozart?

Nicholas Oppenheim London SW6

Sir,

Michael Mannix is not alone: the *Messiah* is dull. *Arrival of the Queen of Sheba*, on the other hand, is so lively that I have it as my mobile ringtone. I actually look forward to incoming calls in spite of odd looks in Waitrose.

Jenny Wright Richmond, Surrey

Book non-signings

Sir,

I have the dubious distinction of having been a no-show at my own book signing ("Book signing no-shows are a humiliating rite of passage", Dec 7). A car fire on the M4 and resulting gridlock meant that by the time I arrived any readers had long since wandered off. On then being approached by a customer, my excitement at a potential sale was dashed when she asked if the car park outside the shop charged on Saturdays, and if so whether I had any change.

Guy Morpuss KC Author of *Five Minds* and *Black Lake Manor*; Farnham, Surrey

Sir,

Sadly, as an author I was never offered a book signing. I approached my nearest bookshop in Muswell Hill to ask if they'd be interested in hosting a launch, stressing that I was a local author. The manager wearily replied: "Sir, everyone in north London is a local author."

David Staples Editor of *Modern Theatres 1950–2020*; London N10

Sir,

Book signings can be stressful for booksellers as well as authors (letters, Dec 8). When running a day-long "sign-athon" of 30 authors of all types at Dillons in London in 1993, I clearly saw how celebrity trumped literary merit. Kingsley Amis, who was asked to sign just five books, could only watch as George Best signed 500, with a queue right round the block.

Julian Rivers Former marketing director, Dillons; Earls Barton, Northants

Sir,

When my wife, Margaret Forster, was alive she did not go to book signings, but I did. Alas, when I thought there was a good queue for me to sign a copy of my latest book, one by one they would say the same thing: "Is your wife here? It was your wife I wanted to meet." When I said no, she was at home, they would turn round and leave without buying a book.

Hunter Davies Ryde, Isle of Wight

Sir,

A book signed in person by the author ensures it will be treasured. My copy of *I Can't Stay Long* was inscribed: "For Mary the ultimate with best wishes Laurie Lee." I have wondered if he omitted a word after "ultimate" and if so what it would be.

Mary Pritchard Richmond, Surrey

And you are?

Sir,
Mary Pritchard's letter (Dec 12) reminds me of a
story PD James told about a book signing in Australia.
A woman placed a book in front of the author and
announced "Emma Chizzitt." James decided to check on
the spelling of the surname. "No," the woman barked,
"how much is it?"

Sir Ian Rankin Edinburgh

Sir,
It would appear that Emma Chizzitt was a devotee
of book signings by visiting British authors, because
exactly the same story ascribed by Sir Ian Rankin (letter,
Dec 13) to PD James was told by Monica Dickens after a
book signing in Sydney in 1964.

John Welford Barlestone, Leics

Sign of greatness

Sir,
While on holiday in Corfu years ago my mother was
carrying the book *Prospero's Cell* by Laurence Durrell.
She spotted his brother Gerald Durrell and to my father's
embarrassment asked him if he would sign it (letters,
Dec 8, 9, 10 & 12). Without a word of protest he took
the book, wrote on the title page, closed the book and
handed it back. The inscription read: "Signed in the
absence of the author by a better one."

Mary Battle London SW18

Touchy-feely art

Sir,
Touching sculpture is essential to its enjoyment and understanding ("Please touch the art to bring back crowds", Dec 30). Forty years ago my husband, the sculptor David Kindersley, stroked a Henry Moore carving at the Kröller-Müller Museum in the Netherlands. An angry attendant told him not to touch the precious exhibit. David explained that the essence of direct carving was the total experience of the senses. The attendant listened, gave an understanding look and answered: "As long as you don't touch the work of art."

Lida Kindersley Cambridge

Staging a walkout

Sir,
I was interested to read about the use of the word "to strike" originating in the Royal Navy and Merchant Navy ("Tide of discontent first rose in the docks", Dec 31). In the theatre we also use the verb "to strike", meaning to disassemble the set or to rid the set of furniture etc. There is another link. In the 18th century the Theatre Royal Drury Lane began using sailors to man the flies, using hemp ropes to winch the sets and cloths on pulleys for the scene changes. They used to communicate through whistles and ever since whistling backstage has been forbidden.

Miranda Fellows Secretary, Drury Lane Theatrical Fund

Lifting the block

Sir,
Carol Midgley (Notebook, Jan 7) regards car washing to be as pointless as ironing tea towels and peeling carrots. All three of these activities have inspired me to overcome writer's block, and are responsible for my 32 published books.

Miller Caldwell Dumfries

Drummer's friend

Sir,
Drummers had a special reason to be grateful to Gina Lollobrigida (obituary, Jan 17). Mumbling her name was a useful template when attempting to drum the rare and tricky seven beats to the bar.

Julien Evans Chesham, Bucks

Hidden talents

Sir,
Further to the letter (Jan 18) on Gina Lollobrigida being of help to drummers facing seven beats in the bar, when I was playing in a concert band the oboe player was struggling with a septuplet, so one of the musicians suggested: "Just think of Gina Lollobrigida." Someone else piped up: "Does she play the oboe?"

Margaret Reed Cuckfield, W Sussex

Signature move

Sir,
I envy the drummers who used Gina Lollobrigida's name to help them measure those tricky seven beats to the bar (letters, Jan 18 & 19). As a brass player, I learnt to fit five quavers into the space of four by simultaneously reciting the word "hippopotamus" in my head.

Alec Gallagher Potton, Beds

La Lollo's legacy

Sir,
It is little realised outside civil engineering circles that Ms Lollobrigida (obituary, Jan 17; letters, Jan 18, 19 & 20) was the inspiration for the Gina gasket used between adjacent sections of submerged tube undersea tunnels. The name arose because of the curvaceous similarity of the profiles when viewed from above.

Peter Mynors London W5

Sir,
Learning to play golf I was told to recite "Seve Ballesteros" while taking my back swing then the follow through. I'm sorry to say I proved to be no competition for the great golfer.

Annette Rigler Edington, Somerset

Band on the pun

Sir,
The Scottish folk circuit generated some good band names ("From Truman Peyote to Sigmund Droid: how pop music fell for puns", Times2, Jan 23). In particular I remember Ceilidh Minogue, the Sensational Jimi Shandrix Experience and, my favourite, Deaf Shepherd.

Peter Lowthian Marlow, Bucks

Sir,
My favourite was a tribute band to Stiff Little Fingers called Rigid Digits.

Charles Murray High Harrington, Cumbria

Sir,
A brilliant Scottish violinist friend of mine went by the name of Yehudi McEwan.

Forrest HC Robertson Milton under Wychwood, Oxon

Mr Darcy's dip

Sir,
Apropos your report "Jane Austen, pride of the meme generation", Jan 27, I always thought the BBC missed a trick in its 1995 production of *Pride and Prejudice*. Garments of the period were made of wool or linen. Mr Darcy would not have leapt into his lake in his clothes, he would have swum in the nude. The unlikely ensuing scenario spoilt the series.

Elizabeth Dineley Shaftesbury, Dorset

Comedy of errors

Sir,
Patrick Kidd's story (TMS, Feb 15) about Sybil
Thorndike's misreading of her script recalls a history
teacher who told me they once read a pupil's essay
describing how Elizabeth I had spent her last years
with the ghost of Mary Queen of Scots hoovering in the
background. A scene worthy of Monty Python.

David Williams Chelmsford, Essex

Censoring Dahl

Sir,
Further to your report "Censoring Roald Dahl 'is like
McCarthyism'", Feb 20, Dr Thomas Bowdler gave
us a useful verb (nothing else) with his edition of
Shakespeare in which "Words and Expressions Are
Omitted which Cannot with Propriety Be Read Aloud
in a Family". It's a bit early but I suggest, as regards
Roald Dahl, that the *Oxford English Dictionary* consider
"puffinise" as its word of the year.

John Sutherland Emeritus Lord Northcliffe professor of
modern English literature, UCL

Sir,
In the light of the Roald Dahl controversy am I now
expected to order an "enormous rascal" when having
afternoon tea at Betty's tea rooms in York or Harrogate?

Dr Roger Norwich Sark, Channel Islands

Censors on campus

Sir,
Thank you for your article on the books removed from courses due to their challenging content. I now have a new summer reading list.

Penny Rowlinson Nantwich, Cheshire

Bobbling baggage

Sir,
As well as gold bars and empty takeaway coffee cups carried by actors that are obviously too light (letters, Feb 18 & 20) there are suitcases that are clearly empty. The only exception seems to be when the suitcase contains a dead body.

David Bloomfield Old Basing, Hants

Milking it

Sir,
Further to the list of heavy objects that actors handle with apparent ease, I was astonished when watching *The Banshees of Inisherin* to see Colin Farrell swing two supposedly full milk churns down from a cart for delivery to the local shop, one in each hand.

Pearl Wheeler Petersfield, Hants

Bogus bump

Sir,

Surely the most obvious example of unrealistic weight in films is the pregnancy bump. Actresses skip around as if gestating a large marshmallow. The only actress I have seen realistically portray the exhausted waddle of late pregnancy is Olivia Colman in *The Night Manager*. But she really was heavily pregnant.

Kate Greenhalgh London SE5

Rowdy audiences

Sir,

Further to your report "Theatre staff voice discontent at drunken audiences", Mar 29, Elizabethan audiences clapped and booed, threw fruit and sometimes climbed on stage. They were rowdy, directly involved with the plays and even replied to soliloquies. They danced when music or a masque was played and thoroughly enjoyed themselves. In many ways we have not changed but the fault of today's drunken audiences is as much attributable to theatres as to those watching. As you report, high ticket prices, "jukebox" musicals and people refusing to pay the exorbitant price for alcohol at the theatre mean they come "pre-loaded". They are as ready to be as involved as Elizabethan audiences. The days of reverential watching are over. Actors who mumble, cannot sing without over-amplification and bring along groupies from their TV careers cannot expect quiet appreciation.

Janice Ketley Englefield Green, Surrey

Sir,

The phenomenon of audiences having altogether too good a time is nothing new. Way back in 1982 I was acting in JP Donleavy's rumbustious comedy *The Beastly Beatitudes of Balthazar B* when my generally acclaimed entrance — naked but for chains, goggles and a motoring cap — failed to make much impact, the audience's delighted attention being focused on the box to the right of the stage, where what used to be called a courting couple were, visibly to some, audibly to all, engaged in the act of procreation. All I could do was to retire upstage somewhat limply until the house manager threw a bucket of water over them. Happy days.

Simon Callow London N8

Sir,

In the first run of Wagner's *Parsifal* at Bayreuth in 1882, an elderly man in one of the boxes insisted on shouting "Bravo" as the flower maidens made their exit in Act II, and was hissed by the rest of the audience (letters, Mar 30). The gentleman was Richard Wagner himself. I am due to see *Parsifal* at Bayreuth in August, and am very tempted to do as Wagner did and see what reaction I get.

Father Richard Duncan Birmingham

Picking nits

Sir,
Further to Sir Michael Morpurgo's warning that "if you start the nitpicking, you never stop" ("We can't rewrite classics to suit modern morals", Apr 24), please let him know that "nit-picking" is hyphenated.

Professor Richard Skinner University of Houston

Library purge

Sir,
When a school where I taught reluctant readers banned and removed Enid Blyton books from the shelves of the school library, I found that wrapping my own much-loved copies in brown paper, and telling my pupils not to let anyone see what they were reading, did wonders for their literacy ("1 in 3 librarians asked to remove books", Apr 21). Might not the removal of other books have a similar "forbidden fruit" effect?

Caroline Lancelyn Green Bebington, Wirral

Sir,
In 55 years of working in a public library I was only once tempted to practise censorship. The book in question was *Lolita*, but I managed to control myself and stay true to the basics of librarianship: no politics, no religion, no morals.

Penelope Tarnowski Isleworth, Middx

Modern
manners

Come dine with me

Sir,
Your archive article "Essentials of a successful dinner party", Apr 27, suggested that "the three indispensable features for a pleasant dinner were a cabinet minister, a duchess and a beautiful woman". In PG Wodehouse's *The Mating Season* Bertie Wooster, referring to his old friend Gussie Fink-Nottle, thinks that "the first essential for an enjoyable dinner party is for Gussie not to be at it".

Peter Lowthian Marlow, Bucks

Sir,
Any successful dinner party in this day and age may indeed involve a cabinet minister, a duchess and a beautiful woman (letter, Apr 30). I recommend combining these attributes to save on the washing-up.

Margaret K Green Odiham, Hants

Sir,
According to a maître d' of a well-known Monégasque hotel, the oil tycoon Nubar Gulbenkian's ideal number for a dinner party was two: "Me and a damn good head waiter."

Robin Wills Hollycombe, W Sussex

Sir,
Further to the letter on the flamboyant financier Nubar Gulbenkian (May 2), when asked why he liked to be chauffeured about London in a black cab, he replied: "I'm told it can turn on a sixpence — whatever that is."

Richard Albright Rottingdean, E Sussex

It could be who?

Sir,
Regarding the news of a record jackpot ("I have a secret . . . we've won £184m", May 20), I recall a few years ago, after reading some tragic stories about the fate of some who have won large sums, I said to my wife, who takes part in the National Lottery, that we had better not win, it would ruin us. She replied: "What do you mean, 'us'?"

Andrew Jones Congleton, Cheshire

Not appy

Sir,
Deborah Ross (Times2, May 26) is right to put the spotlight on parking apps. Computer programmers seem to take no account of people outside their bubble. When mobile phones first came out I was given one for Christmas. The instructions said: "Enter PIN." I kept entering this word until enlightened by a younger person.

Philip Moger East Preston, W Sussex

Love's Jung dream

Sir,
I was delighted to see among the notices in the Forthcoming Marriages today (May 31) the engagement of Petra Jung and Jeremy Love. While knowing neither I can only congratulate them with the hope that they celebrate their happiness by double-barrelling their surnames to become the Jung-Loves.

Robin Gurdon Woodbridge, Suffolk

Name game

Sir,

When I left home for university, I should have told new friends that my name was Judith ("What's in a name? A refusal to conform, study finds", May 31). Unfortunately, I didn't, so now, more than 60 years later, I am still having to tell people that my name has the same emphasis as "Melanie" and not "baloney".

Daloni Judith Peel Bury St Edmunds, Suffolk

Altitude problem

Sir,

Giles Coren writes of his irritation at being overtaken on the near side by a bicycle (Notebook, Jun 7). A similar thing happened to me when I was learning to fly a Tiger Moth over the South Downs: I was overtaken from above by a glider. The cockpit went dark and I looked up to see the underside of the glider only feet away. It was not quite the Tom Cruise head-to-head meeting with the Mig in *Top Gun* but it felt it. I pulled up beside him and made the usual hand signal one uses on these occasions, but he did not reply: he appeared to continue reading his flight manual.

Kevin Lawton Rock, Cornwall

Infantile inflection

Sir,

James Marriott ("The ugly truth about the triumph of twee", Jun 9) overlooks another example of the infantilisation of British society: pronunciation. Adults increasingly struggle to put two consonants together in words. During the pandemic we were constantly told of the dangers posed to "vunnerable" people, encouraged to "reckonise" symptoms and also asked not to go to "hospituws". The word "didn't" regularly becomes the infantile "diddernt", "th" has become "v" in endless words: linguistic infantilisation "whever" we like it or not.

Alistair McGowan Ludlow, Shropshire

Going cash-free

Sir,
Georgina Roberts (Times2, Jun 13) suggests that Gen Z no longer uses cash. May I point out that going without cash is not confined to this age group? I am 72 and never use, or even carry, cash. I use a credit card or, what makes me even less of a dinosaur, Apple Pay on my phone. Not everyone of my age lives in the past.

Dr Barbara Finlay London N20

Sure as eggs

Sir,
I expect there will be a need for cash in the countryside for some time to come (letter, Jun 14; Times2, Jun 13). How else am I going to contribute to the honesty box my neighbour has for payment of his surplus fresh eggs?

Frances Brannon-Rhodes Horsham, W Sussex

Preferred province

Sir,

I empathise with Mark Piggott's sentiments on the reaction to regional accents (Thunderer, Jun 15). As a Lancastrian who worked in London for 20 years in a variety of senior positions, I was often surprised to be asked if I came from Yorkshire. In light of present sensibilities, I now wonder if such comments would be considered microaggressions. To prevent a recurrence, I suggest that before a meeting participants are asked to share their preferred regional or global identity. This would stop individuals like me from being misplaced.

Dr Stephen Twigge Truro

Sir,

Lancastrian Dr Stephen Twigge (letter, Jun 17) considers it a possible microaggression to be asked if he is a Yorkshireman. Surely he should take it as a compliment.

Duncan Webster (Yorkshireman currently on missionary work in Warrington, Cheshire)

Dress for success

Sir,

Further to the article by Hannah Rogers, "Want to dress for success in the sun? Rules are different for men" (news, Jun 17), she is right to put wearing a short-sleeved shirt on the "Don't" list. I was always of the opinion that you never wore a short-sleeved shirt to work unless you were a pilot or an ice-cream seller. Since I was neither, I never did.

Bal Gill York

Sir,

Some 50 years ago Maurice Hudson, a consultant anaesthetist in Harley Street, had his shirt sleeves cut off at the elbow (letter, Jun 20). He then travelled between hospitals and surgeries in his suit with cuffs conventionally visible at the wrist. On arrival he removed his jacket and pulled off his lower sleeves, and was immediately ready for action.

Christine Osborne Ret'd dental surgeon, Sheffield

Noises off

Sir,

Your article "Would you like noise with your dinner, sir?" (Times2, Jun 23), and the advice Gordon Ramsay claims to give his restaurant staff, to put themselves in the shoes of their diners, reminded me of the time we tried the Union Street Café, then one of his newest restaurants. The music was loud and we could barely hear each other. I asked the maître d' if it was possible to turn it down slightly and he said he'd check. He walked over to a nearby table and spoke to someone there. "Tell them to f*** off", came the just audible but unmistakable response from the great man.

Nick Brookes Wimbledon

Thanks a bunch

Sir,

Christopher Smith (letter, June 25) bemoaned loud music in a pub. In my neck of the woods, there is a micro pub with no music. It is also unique, I believe, in having a florist in one corner. However, coming home to my wife with a bouquet in one hand invariably leads to the potentially cryptic comment: "I know where you've been."

John Hemming-Clark Chislehurst, Kent

Go with the show

Sir,

Recovering from a total shoulder replacement operation I was disappointed that clothes continued to slip off the affected shoulder. However, I am somewhat mollified to find (Times2, Jun 22) that it is the height of fashion to reveal one's bra.

Clare Chapman Loughton, Essex

Book at bedtime

Sir,

You report that getting a little one off to sleep is a special soothing time between parents, even if some of the methods might be considered unconventional. When my children were small, I found that five minutes' reading from Mustill and Boyd's *Commercial Arbitration* (second edition) was invariably successful.

Dr Julian Critchlow Head of legal practice, Costigan King solicitors; London EC4

Invented words

Sir,
I very much enjoyed Giles Coren's list of invented words for the various manifestations of anger ("Hangry? No, but I'm absolutely binfuriated", comment, Jul 9). I consider my best effort to be tannoyance — a state of advanced irritability brought on by repeated announcements over a public address system, especially on a long train journey.

Andy Davey Peebles, Scottish Borders

I'm your man

Sir,
On the topic of recognising celebrities (Notebook, Aug 9), I recall pulling up at traffic lights in the mid-1980s and noticing a sports car next to me with music blaring and a rather handsome man at the wheel. Suddenly I realised who it was and called out: "Oh my goodness, you're George Michael!" "Yes," replied the rather handsome man, "I know!"

Anneke Berrill London N1

Spotting the stars

Sir,
On the subject of recognising celebrities (letter, Aug 11), I was out shopping in the Lanes with my colleague, Esther Rantzen, when a woman marched up to her and said: "You're Angela Rippon!" Esther said: "Well, I wasn't this morning."

Norma Herrmann Brighton

Holding hands

Sir,
Janice Turner is right about the value of holding hands (Notebook, Sep 22). The elderly lady taking her seat in front of me on a small aircraft for a stormy flight from a Scottish island introduced herself to the passenger sitting next to her and asked for his first name, saying: "We should be on friendly terms because I am going to be holding your hand for the next half-hour."

David Johnston Athelstaneford, East Lothian

In the flesh

Sir,
Hilary Rose (Times2, Oct 5) might be right that fashion dictates no tights until November. Here in Scotland the weather dictates that no tights until November would result in cold blue legs. I admit I have deferred to the rules of the weather and have embraced the warmth a month early.

Alison Woods Edinburgh

Come on in

Sir,
Regarding your photographic caption "Poised to plunge" (Oct 7), I was swimming with my female friends at Saltburn-by-the-Sea as the sun came up this morning and it was not at all "icy". In fact, the North Sea is now at its warmest after a lovely sunny summer. The local fishermen affectionately call us "the Blue Tits".

Nicola Walker Saltburn-by-the-Sea, N Yorks

We are not appy

Sir,
Regarding Laura Freeman's article on apps (Oct 24), you do not even need to type anything for your phone to know what you are thinking. I mentioned to my daughter that I would move the hen fence to protect the newly seeded lawn. Next day my Facebook page was full of adverts for hen fencing. My daughter thinks my phone must have been in the kitchen with Bluetooth turned on. I found it quite scary, though I quite liked all the pictures of pretty hens that popped up for a while.

Rosemary Carter Lewes, E Sussex

Sir,
Yesterday I had to install a sixth parking app on my phone. Regardless of the serious economic issues of the day, the party that includes a consolidation of parking apps in its manifesto will win my vote.

Richard Bennett Cheltenham, Glos

Name that tune

Sir,
I had to teach a Scout troop the hymn "O God, our help in ages past" for the Remembrance service on Sunday. Unsurprisingly no one knew it, and no one could suggest a warm-up song, so I wildly threw myself into "The wheels on the bus", which they instantly picked up for four loud and gleeful verses. I recommend this to anyone in a similar position.

Andrew MacTavish High Wycombe, Bucks

Meet the parents

Sir,

Further to your report "America's angst at addressing in-laws", Nov 23, when our American son-in-law joined our family he addressed me as "Sir". I asked him to call me Tim. I have since been elevated to "Sir Tim".

Tim Simon London NW1

And you are?

Sir,

My late father-in-law never suggested any name with which to address him ("Meet the parents", letter, Nov 24). Consequently I used to address him as "Excuse me". For example: "Excuse me, could you pass the gravy?"

Simon Buck Ely, Cambs

Ultimate in-law

Sir,

On what to call one's in-laws (letters, Nov 24 & 25), John Betjeman's father-in-law had the answer: "You can't call me Sir Philip — that's too formal. You can't call me Philip — that's too familiar. You had better call me Field Marshal."

Rhidian Llewellyn London SW14

Proletarian poet

Sir,

Field Marshal Sir Philip Chetwode certainly had form
when suggesting names for family members (letter,
Nov 26). Sir John Betjeman told my father that, after
his marriage to Chetwode's daughter, Penelope, the
Field Marshal overheard a servant refer to her as Miss
Penelope. He corrected the servant by saying: "You
cannot call her Miss Penelope any longer; she is Mrs
Bargeman." Sir John had found this most amusing.

Miles Tuely Wootton, Oxon

Lords of lost rings

Sir,

My husband can sympathise with Robert Crampton,
who writes that he has lost two wedding rings (Times2,
Dec 19): my husband is also on Ring No 3. The first lost
one is somewhere at the bottom of the Mediterranean
after a struggle with armbands on a recalcitrant and sandy
two-year-old. He lost the second when called in to do
an emergency caesarean section. Rushing to theatre, he
had no time to go to his locker, so tied Ring No 2 to the
drawstrings of his scrubs. After the baby was delivered
successfully and the stitching-up completed, he went to
change but was dismayed to find that the drawstrings had
come loose, and the ring was missing. The happy new
mum was very sporting about the possibility of playing
host to my late grandmother's beautiful 18-carat-er,

and even suggested, when she returned for a planned caesarean in her next pregnancy, that he have a "rummage around" to see if he could spot it. It was never found.

Suzie Marwood London SW6

Sir,
It's not only men who lose their wedding rings (letter, Dec 21). I lost mine in my daughter's very small kitchen and despite searching high and low we could find no trace of it. The search appeared to be fruitless until my son-in-law, in readiness for a kitchen extension, moved the cooker: as he tilted it forward my ring slid out of a slot at the front. It was undamaged except for being one size smaller after being repeatedly heated and cooled for a couple of years.

Christine Pacione Milton of Campsie, Glasgow

Sir,
A properly heat-treated wedding ring (letter, Dec 24). Joy!

Bob Towers Retired metallurgist, Hamilton, South Lanarkshire

Robot complex

Sir,
I invariably fail to choose the right selection of images on a computer when I am asked to prove that I am not a robot. I am beginning to suspect that I might be a robot.

Dr Phil Stephenson Faculty of Science, Technology, Engineering and Mathematics, Open University

He's still got it

Sir,
I fancy you, Robert, but I am 81 so do I count ("I still want women to fancy me at 58", Robert Crampton, Magazine, Dec 24)?

Brenda Blackburn New Longton, Preston

Certified grown-up

Sir,
Lesley Thomas asks: "What makes you feel like a grown-up?" (Notebook, Dec 24). I long for the day when I can drink a gin and tonic without feeling that I am too young to be doing so. I am 73.

Roger Sykes Sissinghurst, E Sussex

Pearls of wisdom

Sir,
On a bus ride into Leeds I passed two wayside pulpits. The first read, "Make drink your worst enemy", and the second, "Make your worst enemy your best friend".

Melvyn Winburn Leeds

Sir,
The best wayside pulpit I have seen was in Victoria, British Columbia. It read: "Don't despair: even Moses was a basket case."

David Gallop Odiham, Hants

Spit and polish

Sir,

If one of my curates turned up for church with unpolished shoes I sent him home to remedy the imperfection. The priest's shoes are what the parishioner, head bowed, sees when kneeling at the altar rail to receive the blessed sacrament. Scruffy footwear is disrespectful.

The Rev Canon Godfrey Hirst Ansdell, Lancs

Sir,

I was brought up to believe that the job interview was not over till the candidate had turned to leave. This allowed the examiner to determine whether he had bothered to polish the back of his shoes or merely the front.

Mark Haszlakiewicz Goodworth Clatford, Hants

Sir,

No one has yet mentioned polishing under the shoe in front of the heel, ie the part of the sole that has no contact with the ground (letters, Jan 3-5). My Victorian grandfather drilled it into me that it was visible when I took communion. Although I ceased to take communion in my twenties I still polish underneath my dress shoes in his memory.

Mike Wicksteed Caterham, Surrey

Sir,
If only I had followed the wise advice of Mike Wicksteed's Victorian grandfather (letter, Jan 6) and polished that part of the soles of my shoes that had no contact with the ground, I would have avoided the embarrassment of revealing at communion the cartoons I had drawn there of our headmaster.

Christopher Murray Barford St Michael, Oxon

Water over wine

Sir,
Regarding Sathnam Sanghera's Notebook (Jan 16) about a ripe avocado taking precedence over after-work plans, I was reminded of another ingenious excuse, related by our rector in his sermon last Sunday. Apparently one churchgoer said that he could not make this week's service as the communion wine would take him over his weekly limit.

Marilyn Cox Shilton, Oxon

Jungle sign language

Sir,

It should be no surprise that naked apes understand the body language of hairy apes, given that we share 99 per cent of their DNA ("Jungle sign language? It could be in our genes...", news, Jan 25). I will never forget the pursed lips of a chimp of mine that had just attacked my secretary and was refusing to respond to reprimands. Anyone who has worked closely with chimps will know just how close one can become to them, the only divide being their lack of spoken language. Studying other animals is more difficult and a student of animal behaviour must take pains to learn the (quite different) communication systems in each case. Moreover, some species are much more difficult than others. For example, I am fluent in tiger but I only have restaurant lion.

Desmond Morris Athgarvan, Co Kildare

Succinct assessment

Sir,

Further to Carol Midgley's piece "Let's not dilute the f-word" (Times2, Feb 1), when serving as an air liaison officer with the army on exercise on Salisbury Plain, my Land Rover broke down. The corporal driver lifted the bonnet and commented ruefully: "Sir, I think the f***ing f***er's f***ed." It seemed to me a concise and accurate assessment of the situation.

Peter Butcher Group captain RAF (ret'd), Shrewsbury

Out of pocket

Sir,
Emma Duncan (Notebook, Feb 7) may feel that her rights are affronted by the lack of properly designed pockets in women's garments. However, OfPock's first investigation must be into the fashion industry's propensity to believe that only right-handed women deserve a pocket, leaving the left-handed woman pocketless.

Gillian Dunkeld London N2

Sir,
As annoying as the absence of pockets on women's trousers and skirts (letters, Feb 8) is the provision of breast pockets on shirts and tops. What do designers expect us to carry in them? Phone? Cigarettes and lighter? A row of pens?

Sheila Lamisere Fisher, Australian Capital Territory

Sir,
Further to the letters about pockets on women's garments (Feb 8 & 11), my many years in the rag trade taught me that the more details there were on an item of clothing — pockets, epaulettes, button-down collars, pleats etc — the more people were employed in factories. Conversely, we were sometimes told by the manufacturers that if we reduced these features, employees might be laid off. The actual purpose and placement of random pockets was rarely considered.

Sue Brandon Warlingham, Surrey

Sir,

I am very much in favour of breast pockets on both sides of shirts and tops. Since the pandemic my bras remain discarded somewhere at the back of the wardrobe. Double-breasted pockets are great for disguising nipples but nature's gravitational pull requires the pockets to be longer as time goes on.

Betty Pearson Christchurch, New Zealand

Regal hole in sock

Sir,

Your photograph (Feb 9) of the King at a mosque in east London shows a hole in his sock. André Maurois, in his *Advice to a Young Man Travelling to England* (1938), describes the Duke of Devonshire's "grey woollen toe emerging from a longish hole in his right boot" as "really ducal" and advises: "In England, clothes should not be too careful, nor shoes too new."

Christopher McKane London N1

Toe in the market

Sir,

A hole in a sock, sometimes called a potato, is a sign of our shared humanity. When selling our home in the Scottish Borders we approached three estate agents for quotes and selected one from a rather posh office in Edinburgh. Its agent asked: "Why did you choose our company?" My wife replied: "When you took off your muddy shoes to view our house you had a hole in your sock."

David Jeffrey West Malvern, Worcs

Kernel of an idea

Sir,
Matthew Parris's difficulty in identifying his blue coat (Notebook, Feb 8) might have been eased if he always carried something identifiable in the pocket. All my working life, I have carried a walnut in the hip pocket of my jacket and it has never let me down. After 40 years of working in town, I still have both.

Anthony Collins Edgbaston, Birmingham

Sir,
Anthony Collins (letter, Feb 10) carries a walnut in his pocket so that he can identify his coat. Another idea is to keep a potato in your coat pocket, like Leopold Bloom in *Ulysses*.

Pauline Trapp Banwell, Somerset

Aching to talk

Sir,

I enjoyed Emma Duncan's report of her parents' rule that older folks' discussion of health issues should be limited to Fridays (Notebook, Feb 20). A friend of mine has a different rule: on meeting up, ten minutes is the maximum time permitted for an "organ recital".

Chris Hickey Berkhamsted, Herts

To have and to hold

Sir,
Further to your report "It's no longer indecent to propose without parents' permission" (May 1), I thought I had a rather good relationship with (hopefully) my future father-in-law, but when I said that I had a question I needed to ask him he looked horrified. Perplexed but resolute, I asked for the hand of his daughter. His relief was practically explosive as he said: "Thank goodness! I thought you wanted to borrow my tools."

Colonel AB Barton Colchester, Essex

Food
and
drink

Hard cheese

Sir,
Not all English cheeses are worthy of celebrating
("British artisans breaking the mould", May 10).
Choke-dog, the Isle of Wight cheese made from skimmed
milk, was so notoriously hard that the recipient of one
sent as a present apparently failed to recognise it as food.
Cutting a hole through the middle with some difficulty, he
is said to have used it successfully as a grindstone.

Jacquie Pearce Cowes, Isle of Wight

Planetary cress

Sir,
Why all the fuss about growing cress in moon dust
("Moon dust heralds a giant leek for mankind", May 13)?
Many of us grew cress on pieces of blotting paper. Cress
will grow in almost anything.

David Slinn Newport-on-Tay, Fife

Food glorious food

Sir,
What a miserable idea, to have all your meals between
6am and 3pm ("No more food after 3pm to call time on
weight gain", Jun 3). For a working person this would
mean somehow finding time to cook and eat a main meal
in the middle of the day without the benefit of wine or
relaxation, and would leave rather an empty evening
ahead. Of course our hunter-gatherer ancestors "did not

have continuous access to a food supply" but who wants to live like them?

Madeline Macdonald Knebworth, Herts

Senior servings

Sir,
Jean Inson (letter, Jun 10) raises the idea of restaurants having smaller portions for older or smaller appetites. Such a thing exists in Germany — known as the *Seniorenteller* menu. Here in Britain you can try to order from the children's menu, of course, but you may be thought a cheapskate.

Lesley Bright Haywards Heath, W Sussex

Foodie freeloaders

Sir,
Margaret Askew laments that it is always the very wealthy who receive freebies when dining out (letter, Jun 11). When I was a restaurant critic, several chefs and proprietors told me of a known cabal of A-listers who would always pay for their lavish meals with a cheque — in the certain knowledge it would not be cashed but instead framed and prominently displayed in the restaurant.

Joseph Connolly London NW3

Delicious venison

Sir,

I thoroughly endorse any move to include wild venison in the British diet and especially that of the introduced and invasive muntjac deer ("Booming deer population puts venison steaks at the top of the menu", Jun 25). I first became familiar with the muntjac in the 1970s when the carcass of one was brought into the museum where I was keeper of natural history after it had had a fatal encounter with a motor vehicle. After our taxidermist had skinned it I removed a leg and took it home to cook. It was delicious.

Henry Middleton Maidstone, Kent

Half-baked theory

Sir,

Surely thrice-baked biscuit-rolls (letter, Jul 13) are triscuits not biscuits?

Pat Notley Hunston, Suffolk

Smelling trouble

Sir,

Tony Turnbull's advice to use the "sniff test" ("Why the food editor ignores 'best before' dates," Jul 19) is of little use to those of us deprived of our sense of smell or taste by Covid-19. Without the ability to taste or season, every meal is a venture into the unknown, for cook and guests alike. Is every visit to the fridge now to be a game of Russian roulette?

Christine Michael Shipston-on-Stour, Warks

Inventive genius

Sir,

Max Hastings may like to know (Notebook, Jul 19) that the product scientist who came up with the concept and developed the recipe for the Mars ice-cream bar was Dan Jacoby, a brilliant young man we nicknamed the mad professor. He not only had the idea but developed the recipe and enthusiastically persuaded all the doubters, including me, in finance, that we could sell the product for a high enough price to justify investment. Sadly, Dan died in 2015, but in his last year a few of his former Mars colleagues had lunch with him to reminisce and pay tribute to his genius. His legacy is a product that is regularly in (and out of) my freezer.

Bob Beveridge Chairman, PastMasters Mars Confectionery 1981-93

Nugget of wisdom

Sir,

Further to Sathnam Sanghera's research on overseas branches of McDonald's (Notebook, Aug 1), when I lived in Rome a few years ago I found the fast-food chain's city map invaluable. Although I made no use of the details of McDonald's branches located around the Eternal City, the map was to a convenient scale and contained most of the information I wanted. Moreover, as it was free, I didn't need to worry if my copy got wet, torn or lost — I could always get another from the branch around the corner from where I worked.

Kieran O'Kelly Andover, Hants

Date of milking

Sir,

I agree that "best before" dates should be abolished (news, Aug 1) but it would be useful for products to be marked with the date that the cow was milked, the vegetables harvested, the bread baked, and the fish caught etc. This would allow well-informed purchase in the shop and consumption in the correct order at home.

Lord Terrington London SW4

Saving water

Sir,

On ideas to save water, I am surprised no one has mentioned Quentin Crisp's advice that one only needs to wash up dishes after eating fish. For other foods the taste of the previous meal serves to enhance that of the present one, with fish at the end of the chain. Medical students' advance on this was that even this washing could be avoided or delayed if the next meal was fish too.

Anthony Cohn London NW4

Dirt, what dirt?

Sir,

Quentin Crisp (letter, Aug 5) also asserted that there is no need to do any housework as, after the first four years, the dirt doesn't get any worse — advice I have followed assiduously in the room I call my study.

Crawford Gillan Ipswich, Suffolk

Pass the mustard

Sir,
Not only is there going to be a shortage of French and Swiss cheese ("Heatwave to make French cheese whey more pricey", Aug 8), there is no Dijon mustard to be had in France (news & leading article, Aug 10). Perhaps Parisian dinner guests will start bringing a small jar of Maille rather than a bottle of wine. I'm wondering whether my catering-size tin of Colman's might pay for the winter fuel bill rise.

Suzie Marwood London SW6

Sir,
Further to your letter about the Dijon mustard shortage, a friend of mine has just set off to his property in Aveyron with 22 jars of Maille in his car, all at the request of his deprived French neighbours.

Peter Cartledge Tetchill, Shropshire

Tea up

Sir,
I was so horrified when I read Hilary Rose's article about making tea with a teabag that I knocked over my mug of tea, scattering the rich, brown builder's liquid and the wet tea leaves from the bottom of the mug all over the newspaper ("Here's the right way to make a tea", Times2, Aug 16). True northerners would never think to use a bag, scorched or otherwise.

Paulette Smith Accrington, Lancs

Time for a brew

Sir,

I needed comfort and reassurance after reading Hilary Rose's description of making tea (Times2, Aug 16) and then your correspondent's reaction to it (Aug 17). Luckily my brew (made with leaves and enough for four cups, with the remainder used to soak the fruit for a Yorkshire tea loaf) was ready to be poured from the pot.

Christine Hiskey Wells-next-the-Sea, Norfolk

Sir,

Having spent my entire career in the tea trade I have tasted teas from all over the world. I have never encountered a "scorched" teabag described by Hilary Rose but have certainly had the misfortune to be confronted by teas that were burnt, fusty, chesty, flat and fruity. As for adding a good slug of milk while your teabag brews ... oh dear, oh dear!

Simon Bowes Tarrant Keyneston, Dorset

Sir,

In answer to a comment from one of your readers as to what is "chesty" tea (letter, Aug 18), in the days when tea was packed in chests the chests were lined with paper and foil to keep the tea fresh. Occasionally, if the chests were not properly prepared, the wood of the chest gave off a cheesy odour that the tea picked up. This applied particularly to teas from India and were referred to by tasters as being cheesy or chesty.

Simon Bowes Tarrant Keyneston, Dorset

Different kettle

Sir,
I was mildly interested to learn that Tom Kerridge (Times2, Aug 18) cooks for George and Amal Clooney but wildly intrigued to learn he also takes part in an initiative "teaching children how to make an omelette in a kettle". Well! It beats making a white sauce in a pan any day.

Gilly Hendry Gullane, East Lothian

Family recipes

Sir,
Giorgio Locatelli says that Brits don't pass down recipes as the Italians do (Times2, Sep 22). My wife copied out all her recipes three times to give to her children, many of them passed to her from their grandmother. I often hear, "Mum, I made such and such but it didn't taste like yours" to which the reply is, "Ah that's because I don't follow the recipe".

Mark Ward Sandleheath, Hants

Golden Yorkshire

Sir,
If Carol Midgley ("Yorkshire padding", Notebook, Oct 8) ventured over the Pennines into God's Own Country she would find that the only way to eat Yorkshire puddings is on their own as a first course. I never, ever serve them with meat and vegetables. We eat them with onion gravy,

perhaps a little horseradish sauce or some Yorkshire salad. They deserve to be admired on their own.

Marion Moverley Easingwold, N Yorks

The full Yorkshire

Sir,
Marion Moverly (letter, Oct 11) has too limited a vision of the glorious Yorkshire pudding. As a child in North Yorkshire I had Sunday lunch with a farming family at which the Yorkshire came on for all three courses: first with gravy, second with the meat and veg, and third dressed in a splash of milk and sugar as pudding.

Gordon Johnson Former president, Wolfson College, Cambridge

Yorkshire economy

Sir,
My father, a born-and-bred Yorkshireman, who always ate his Yorkshire pudding (letters, Oct 10-13) before the main course, told us children that the reason this practice arose was because it filled up hungry tummies so that less meat, which was expensive, was required.

Anne Taylor Epsom, Surrey

Puddings aplenty

Sir,

I am a born and bred Yorkshire lass who as a child also ate her Yorkshire pudding before the main course, with gravy (letter, Oct 14), but also ate Yorkshire pudding with jam after the main meal if still hungry.

Val Hepplewhite Bath

Keep calm and eat

Sir,

Giles Coren writes with affection of Simpson's Tavern at $38^{1/2}$ Cornhill in the City of London ("Scrooge is alive and operating from Bermuda", Nov 5). For many years my partners and I had a regular lunchtime table at the Tavern. Periodically the chimney over the grill caught fire. On these occasions "Mr Sid", the manager, insisted that we continue with our lunch, assuring us that there was no danger and that it saved the expense of employing a chimney sweep. One such fire attracted the fire brigade and we were ordered to evacuate the building. We cheerfully ignored this instruction and continued with our lunch.

Patrick Griggs Ongar, Essex

Banana bonanza

Sir,

On the subject of the banana drought of the Second World War (Feedback, Nov 12), at the age of seven I was bewildered by the almost delirious excitement of the grown-ups in our village hall in Hertfordshire in 1944 when the first prize in a raffle was one banana. Mother whispered to me that it had been smuggled to England in a pilot's flying jacket. Her ticket was not a winner and I had to wait until I was at secondary school before I had my first taste, served in slices.

Christopher South Little Chesterford, Essex

Respect this fruit

Sir,

Helen Rumbelow is right to be enthusiastic about ackee (Notebook, Nov 21). The standard Jamaican dish is saltfish and ackee, although Usain Bolt is perfectly right to enthuse about ackee for breakfast. However, if you eat ackee before it is ripe it is poisonous. You need to wait for the pinky-red husk to burst open: the yellow ackee inside will then be fine. But if you pick the pod early and break it open to eat the unripe ackee, it can be fatal. In my time in Jamaica there were regular reports in the paper of children having died from eating the ackee too soon.

David Shepherd Woodstock, Oxon

English haggis

Sir,
Perhaps Scotland need not worry about the origin of the haggis ("Sorry Scotland but haggis is an English dish", Jan 30). The given recipe of grated meat (or more usually offal) cooked in pig's caul is the classical faggot of industrial Middle England. Caul is the fatty netlike greater omentum of an animal. Haggis, on the other hand, is grated offal cooked in a pig's stomach.

Percy Carpenter Aldridge, West Midlands

Sir,
Further to Percy Carpenter's mention of the "classical faggot of industrial Middle England" (letter, Jan 31), my father was known for his faggots, made in the Bloxwich area of the West Midlands. Customers would bring their own basins every Friday and buy faggots, along with mushy peas and gravy made by my Mum. He sold 200 faggots every week at a price of 6d each. An early and very tasty form of takeaway.

Sue Barnfield West Bromwich, West Midlands

Sir,
Perhaps it is best that an Englishman should not comment on haggis. Contrary to Percy Carpenter's view, it is not cooked in a pig's stomach but in that of a sheep.

Callum Beaton St Martin's, Guernsey

Sir,

Callum Beaton is right that haggis is conventionally cooked in a sheep's stomach (letters, Feb 1 & 2). However, each December our Selkirk butcher kindly supplies me with a couple of ox bungs (or beef caps, as they are known in England) to allow me my annual filling of haggis bags from the cooked "lights" (lungs, liver, heart) along with other tastier bits of lamb and beef. And fat. Sold washed and salted, these lengths of bovine intestine are not only convenient for the butcher but also for the amateur haggis-maker as, when filled, they fit perfectly into a fish kettle.

David Macdonell Lilliesleaf, Scottish Borders

Sir,

The principle of haggis — an animal's stomach stuffed with its own chopped offal and boiled — was already ancient in Britain 600 years ago (letters, Jan 31, Feb 1–3). Several medieval English manuscripts have a haggis recipe, with the oldest thought to date from about 1420–30. Why no early recipes from Scotland? Simply because we have no medieval Scottish cookery manuscripts. Scots certainly already ate it around 1500, when William Dunbar described a poetic rival gaping greedily for "ane haggeis".

Victoria Solt Dennis Gillingham, Kent

Fast-food leftover

Sir,
Regarding your story about the McDonald's playing classical music ("A little night music to repel McYobs", Feb 11), I used to go regularly to McDonald's in Bournemouth town centre and was surprised not only to hear classical music but to have a well known broadsheet to read (The Daily Telegraph). I asked the manager one day why his outlet was so highbrow. "We have no choice about the music," he said, "but we have all the newspapers in the morning — it's just that all the others get stolen."

Sally Wilton Bournemouth

Store of knowledge

Sir,
I see that the advice now is to keep avocados at room temperature (until ripe, then in the fridge). I generally find that the interval between "rock hard" and "rotten", ie the time when they are judged to be edible, is approximately half an hour ("Chill out, it's now safe to store potatoes in the fridge", news, Feb 27). I long for a fail-safe way of gauging the ripeness of an avocado.

Diana Lock Southsea, Hants

Sir,
There is a simple way to tell when to put an avocado in the fridge (letter, Feb 28): squeeze it at both ends. If there is any movement, put it in the fridge and eat it within three days.

Julian Turner Westward Ho, Devon

Sir,
It is indeed a problem gauging when avocados are ripe. Sadly the only solution is to always buy at least one extra, to replace the inevitable rotten infiltrator.

Sally Causton Bristol

Tomato tourists

Sir,
Given the paucity and rationing of tomatoes, cucumbers and peppers etc, a group of us have arranged a ferry trip to the markets of Calais to replenish our fridges and have a day out. Unable to call it a "booze cruise", we have renamed it a "salad safari".

Stephen Pritchard Eynsham, Oxon

Delicious daffs

Sir,
Martin Samuel asks, "Who eats daffodils?", Notebook, Mar 3. During the war my father, an ARP warden, liked a boiled onion for his supper. My mother's sister lived in Liverpool, where she obtained items on the black market. Imagine my parents' delight to receive a parcel of "onions" from her. The next week my aunt wrote in her weekly letter: "I hope you got the daffodils planted." My father lived to be 84.

Anne Hulse Great Asby, Cumbria

Squirrel surprise

Sir,
There's nothing new about eating squirrel meat, it has been gradually gaining popularity for years ("Up the Reds", leading article, Mar 23). In 2019 I visited Hexham on market day, where the butcher's stall was doing good business selling saddles of squirrel, all neatly packaged, each bearing a helpful safety label: "Warning: may contain nuts."

Victoria Solt Dennis Gillingham, Kent

Sir,
My wife and I served up homemade squirrel pâté for supper years ago and our guests loved it. One guest asked the nature of the dish and there was a lull in the conversation when they learnt they had just eaten grey squirrel, until one lady piped up: "How wonderful. I haven't had squirrel since we were in Burma."

Vernon Mann Beckington, Somerset

Sir,
As internees in a Japanese camp in the 1940s, my family and I were once obliged to eat not grey squirrels (leading article, Mar 13; letters, Mar 14) but greyhounds from the Sassoon family kennels in Shanghai. I don't know how the taste compares but the legs were certainly bigger.

Bob Ridley Dinnington, Tyne and Wear

Sir,

Had Victoria Solt Dennis (letter, Mar 14) visited the Hexham area 30 years earlier she could have come to our pub, The Manor House Inn, on the A68 and enjoyed squirrel stuffed with hazelnuts. The squirrels were supplied by one of our regular guests, the splendid Mr Jones, who brought the squirrels "fresh from Shropshire" in a coolbox every Monday evening. They were delicious but a bit bony.

Anthony Pelly Bishop's Nympton, Devon

The full English

Sir,

I was disappointed to read the calls for hash browns to be banished from the full English (news, Mar 31). Hash browns can offer a gluten-free alternative to toast and can be baked as well as fried, freeing up space on the hob. While they may not have a place at the core of the fry-up, it is surely time to accept the reality of a two-tier arrangement, in which hash browns have become a bone-fide opt-in, popular with younger generations and in continental Europe.

Edward Robinson London N1

Sir,

The plate of food you depicted is a mixed grill, definitely not a full English. A traditional full English needs bacon and egg and very little more. And no to toast — toast is for the marmalade, to be enjoyed with a cup of tea after the main event.

Viv Mercer Southport, Merseyside

Sir,

The indomitable Mrs Beeton's breakfast menus included eggs, sausage, bacon, and toast, along with more exotic items such as soused mackerel, veal cake, pressed beef, kidneys and game pie. She made no mention of black pudding or mushrooms and certainly not of baked beans or hash browns. Neither of these American upstarts can possibly be considered part of the English breakfast.

Ian Pearce Great Ayton, North Yorkshire

Sir,

Where is the fried bread?

Roger Cooper Northwood, Middx

Sir,

I note with interest the ingredients of an ideal English breakfast. While I would wish all the list of ingredients on my morning plate, I would have to add delectable white pudding.

Enda Cullen Armagh

Sir,

A cooked breakfast is not complete without a Staffordshire oatcake. Ask anyone in Stoke-on-Trent.

Andre Evans Linkinhorne, Cornwall

Sir,

One item seems to have been forgotten. Before the last war provincial hotels would serve their cooked morning fare with a glass of ale, a custom probably stemming from coaching inns and perhaps overdue for a revival.

Martin Grindley Westcliff-on-Sea, Essex

Politics, royalty and the church

Empire strikes back

Sir,

James Marriott says that, when reading Jan Morris's *Pax Britannica* trilogy about the history of the British Empire (Notebook, May 16), he was "struck by the generational gulf in understanding that lies underneath the culture war about Britain's imperial legacy". Is Morris outdated, as Marriott claims? Possibly. Out of fashion? Certainly. Wrong? Not necessarily.

Richard Hunt Gunnerside, N Yorks

Cross purposes

Sir,

You quote Alan Sked as saying that not long ago Glasgow University warned its theology students that a course on Christ ended "with a violent episode called the Crucifixion". I was always taught that things ended with a triumphant episode called the Resurrection. Perhaps times have changed.

James Gladstone Edinburgh

Grown in Britain

Sir,

Farmers have complained that some people are happy to live off benefits rather than pick crops. At the same time Prince Andrew is looking for a job and to be accepted back by the public. This is an ideal opportunity for him to lead by example: I am sure the chance to pick onions with a member of the royal family would encourage other workers to come forward, and I doubt the farmer would mind if Andrew wore one of his many uniforms.

Alan Parsons Leeds

Partygate politics

Sir,
Some time ago I applied to join the Conservative Party's candidate list. I remember being slightly surprised at being asked: "Have you done anything that could embarrass our party?" I answered "No". I now know I gave the wrong answer.

Tim Russell London W12

Political pool

Sir,
I was appalled by the choice of a picture of Penny Mordaunt in a blue swimsuit next to her fully clothed, mostly male counterparts ("Runners and riders in race to become next leader", Jul 8). As women are already underrepresented and disadvantaged in politics, I suggest that next time they are all photographed in suits, as no one should be subjected to those men in budgie smugglers.

Isla Flett Twickenham, Middx

Good chaps

Sir,
Clare Foges, quoting the historian Peter Hennessy, refers to the "good chap" theory. This theory, to which the cabinet adheres unanimously, simply states that a good chap doesn't tell a good chap what a good chap ought to know.

Jonathan Lynn Co-writer, *Yes Minister* and *Yes Prime Minister*, New York

Church and states

Sir,
The Bishop of Leeds has a valid point ("Let Russia keep Donbas to achieve peace, says bishop", News, Jun 24). Extending the same principle, I suggest he cede part of his diocese to the Archbishop of York, to forestall any possible land grabs by his more powerful neighbour.

The Rev Janet Fife Whitby, N Yorks

Tetchy king

Sir,
Regarding our new king's tetchiness ("King loses temper in a flash, say staff", Sep 26), in the early 1990s I reviewed an exhibition of royal watercolours at Holyrood Palace for *The Times*. While praising Queen Victoria's efforts I made some mildly scathing comments about those of the Prince of Wales. Imagine my astonishment to be telephoned on my home telephone number by Dickie Arbiter, the prince's press secretary, to be informed as to

how upset his employer had been. I dithered emotionally between feeling shocked and honoured.

Andrew Gibbon-Williams Upper Beeding, W Sussex

Covering the news

Sir,
Lesley Russell (letter, Oct 4) uses old copies of *The Times* to prevent draughts. So did I when I was homeless in London for a week in June 1972. Bishop Mervyn Stockwood of Southwark had decreed that a few fit curates should spend a few days on the streets of central London to gain first-hand experience of being homeless. I was selected, and with the £3 I was given bought copies of *The Times* to read during the day and to cover myself as a paper blanket at night as I lay on a bench in Victoria Embankment Gardens. It provided both sleep and security.

Canon Brian Stevenson West Peckham, Kent

Well-read feet

Sir,
My father didn't really approve of central heating. Instead, he relied on *The Times* to keep him warm (letters, Oct 4-6). Sitting at his desk with his feet in a large cardboard box, he stuffed it full with old copies of *The Times*, saved specifically for that purpose. Great for him, but less helpful for the rest of us.

Tom Foulkes Fleet, Hants

Member for Mars

Sir,

You report that the android Ai-Da will be the first non-sentient being to contribute to British democracy when it addresses the House of Lords next week (report, Oct 7). Where do I begin?

Marc Porter Wellow, Hants

Coronation-lite

Sir,

Your leading article ("Pomp and Circumstance", Oct 13) says that the coronation will last only one hour in contrast to the three-hour ceremony of 1953. The coronation of the nine-year-old Edward VI on February 20, 1547, was shortened, in recognition of the King's youth, from 12 hours to a mere seven.

Ross Hadley Hitchin, Herts

Crowning moment

Sir,

There were 8,000 people in Westminster Abbey for the 1953 coronation, so a large choir of 350 singers was necessary. The trebles consisted of the full choirs of Westminster Abbey, St Paul's Cathedral, St George's Chapel, Windsor, the Chapel Royal, selected choristers from cathedrals and colleges around the country and 20 boys from the Royal School of Church Music.

There were only 19 women in the choir, and they were all from the dominions. This greatly upset British female singers. After the coronation the Archbishop of Canterbury, Geoffrey Fisher, and the director of music, Sir William McKie, discussed it at length. Their solution was to recommend that in a future coronation there should be no female singers at all.

James Wilkinson Westminster Abbey chorister 1951-55; author, *The Queen's Coronation*

British to the core

Sir,
Further to Emma Duncan's piece "The British citizenship test takes the cake", Notebook, Nov 14, the definitive test for awarding citizenship should surely be: "When did you last play Pooh sticks?"

John Pitts Penarth, Vale of Glamorgan

Brotherly love

Sir,
My brother and I still scream and shout at each other ("Harry deepens rift with 'screaming' William" jibe, Dec 16). I put it down to immaturity. We're in our sixties.

Nigel Webb Appledore, Kent

Kim's numeracy

Sir,

The PM's plan to make maths compulsory until the age of 18 (news, Jan 4; letters, Jan 5 & 6) may reduce the future number of innumerate politicians, who invariably describe the growth rate in any activity as "exponential" without understanding what it means. The habit has even extended to North Korea, where Kim Jong-un recently announced his intention to enlarge his nuclear arsenal exponentially. One wonders what he means.

Seymour Redstone London SW15

Just add whisky

Sir,

The King is quite right about the delights of peaty water ("William didn't tell me he was getting married, Harry claims", Jan 11). At the Hill House in Helensburgh there is a room designed for the chatelaine to do her flower arrangements: there are three taps above the sink — for hot, cold and spring water.

Matthew Hudson Helensburgh, Argyll & Bute

Nott Cott's comfort

Sir,
I was amused by the Duke of Sussex's complaint that Nottingham Cottage in the grounds of Kensington Palace was "constructed for small people, humans of a bygone era" ("Cottage had Ikea lamps and felt like 'frat house'", Jan 12). My father, Philip Hay, lived there for ten years until his death in 1986. He was 6ft 4in and was entirely happy and comfortable there, even by the standards of humans of today. He had worked for the royal family for nearly 40 years, which he regarded as a privilege, as he did living at Nottingham Cottage. He never complained about anything — but he had spent three and a half years as a prisoner of war on the Burma railway, so probably knew a little about physical and mental discomfort.

Andrew Hay London SW6

Hall of mummies

Sir,
I am surprised that "mummy" is now deemed unacceptably colonialist ("Museums scrap 'mummy' label over colonial legacy", Jan 23), particularly given its roots in the Arabic language of the often overlooked labourers and archaeologists responsible for excavating many of Egypt's tombs. Perhaps someone should tell the Egyptian Ministry of Antiquities? Its recently opened Royal Mummies' Hall — the centrepiece of the National Museum of Egyptian Civilisation — will need rebranding.

Max Bruges Cairo

Robed in frippery

Sir,

Matthew Parris is rightly outraged by the vestments shop in his Notebook (Feb 1). It is high time the Church of England called a stop to this ridiculous expense. Have we forgotten that it was those seeking to kill Jesus who wore this ecclesiastical frippery? As far as we know the Lord dressed like an ordinary bloke and it is time we did too.

The Rev Canon Andrew Wingfield Digby Witney, Oxon

Sir,

Matthew Parris (Notebook, Feb 1) and the Rev Canon Andrew Wingfield-Digby (letter, Feb 2) may have overlooked something when commenting on clerical attire and ecclesiastical accoutrements displayed in a Westminster shop: that they were made to enhance the worship of God.

The Rev Prebendary Nigel Jackson-Stevens
Barnstaple, Devon

Non-gender prayers

Sir,

The question of gender attribution in matters spiritual is not new ("Priests want prayers to make 'Our Father' gender-neutral", Feb 8). Ogden Nash was prescient when he wrote: "I like to watch the clouds roll by/ And think of cherubs in the sky/ But when I think of cherubim/ I don't know if they're her or him."

Andrew Colvin London W13

Sir,
The Church of England is hardly in the vanguard to
make our Father gender-neutral. Graffiti at Waterloo
Station decades ago pronounced: "God is Black".
Underneath someone had added: "I know she is."

Jamie Berry London SW1

We simply must go

Sir,
Further to the graffiti about God at Waterloo Station
(letter, Feb 9), I recall seeing a large sign at Liverpool
Street Station that read: "Harwich for the Continent."
Underneath someone had scrawled: "and Bournemouth
for the Incontinent."

John Wallinger Upton Grey, Hants

Train of thought

Sir,
Stations are a rich source of graffiti (letters, Feb 10 & 11).
In the late 1970s British Rail started recruiting female
train drivers for the first time. The posters often had added
to them the slogan: "Women's right to choo-choos."

Bruce Hunt Linton, Cambs

Tuber town

Sir,
My favourite graffito (letters, Feb 10, 11 & 13) is the addition to a farmer's roadside notice "POTATOES", reading "twinned with Pommes de Terre".

Sarah Parton Loughborough, Leics

Tuber bellies

Sir,
The letter on potatoes (Feb 14) reminded me of a large hoarding at a farm entrance off the A12 years ago, when the Tutankhamun exhibition was on at the British Museum. The notice simply said: "POTATOES. TOOT AND COME IN."

Anthony Osmond-Evans Tilbury Juxta Clare, Essex

Sir,
My favourite graffito was on a Tube poster promoting a visit to the Tower of London with a beaming image of Henry VIII, a balloon from his mouth reading: "Return to Tower Hill please." Underneath someone had written: "And a single for the wife."

David Martin Lyneham, Wilts

Spy balloon puzzle

Sir,
The best way to quickly find the origin of these balloons
("British jets are ready to shoot down spy balloons",
Feb 14) is to locate the label and see if it says "Made
in China".

Dr Paul Truelove Cromer, Norfolk

Get to the point

Sir,
Harry Wallop endorses Dominic Raab's preference for
brevity ("I'll keep this brief: Dominic Raab is right to
insist on short, clear memos", Times2, Feb 17). When
Norman Tebbit arrived at the Department for Trade and
Industry in 1983 he changed the style of submissions,
insisting that the issue was stated first followed
immediately by the official's recommendation. He said
that, if he agreed with the recommendation, he did
not want to read more. This, of course, annoyed civil
servants, who wanted to ensure the minister understood
the issue, but it certainly speeded up decisions.

Ian Jones Lingfield, Surrey

Brief encounter

Sir,

When President Reagan became exasperated by the amount of reading material crossing his desk (letter, Feb 21) he asked his staff to submit only one-page memos with four sections: 1. The problem 2. The facts 3. The arguments 4. The recommendations. When I was promoted to run a large department I tried this on my staff but they were underwhelmed.

Ian Elliott Hathersage, Derbyshire

Computer says no

Sir,

Thirty years ago I worked for Telewest, the cable television and telephone company. Sir Bernard Ingham (obituary, Feb 25) was a customer wanting to move his billing date. In those days the system issued monthly bills in alphabetical order by surname, putting Sir Bernard's billing date in the middle of the month. When this was explained, he replied: "Mrs White, are you telling me we can put a man on the moon but you can't move my billing date?" Needless to say, we moved his billing date.

Bonnie White Wells, Somerset

Following the rules

Sir,
Several years ago I was fined for not paying the London congestion charge. I wrote three letters complaining that as a resident of northern England I had no knowledge of the charge and the fine was thus unfair. The final response from the Greater London Authority was signed by the mayor of the time, Boris Johnson. He explained that it was my responsibility to find out the rules and abide by them, and that lack of knowledge was no defence. I accepted this and paid.

Chris O'Flaherty Preston

Parish protest

Sir,
Emma Thompson is to be congratulated for speaking the truth to power ("Church needs to fund more vicars to reverse decline", Thunderer, Apr 10). I retired ten years ago but am helping to support five country parishes. Meanwhile, the Diocese of Coventry has appointed an evangelist on £50,000 a year who is "not expected to work weekends".

The Rev Canon A James Canning Coventry

Bonfire of beacons

Sir,

Further to your report "Brecon loses its Beacons to go green" (Apr 17), perhaps we could also rename the frequent congestion either side of the Brynglas tunnels on the M4. How about *tagfa draffig wenwynig* (toxic traffic jam), as an acknowledgement of their contribution to air pollution? And where on earth are we going to find a carbon-neutral dragon?

Martin Jeeves Cardiff

Political talent pool

Sir,

There has always been a tendency in the Conservative Party to prefer local candidates, all other things being equal ("Too much localism gives us second-rate MPs", Apr 25; letter, Apr 26), but very frequently other things are not equal. In my own interview, for Burton in 1973, the first question I was asked was what were my links to the constituency. I had to answer "none". I was then asked what I knew about the brewing industry. I had to answer "nothing". Then I was asked what I knew about farming. Again I had to answer "nothing". "I think we must choose him," the president told the selection committee. "He is the first honest candidate we have interviewed!" Sadly, although I was not local, Margaret Thatcher did not think I was first-rate enough to invite me to join any of her ministries.

Sir Ivan Lawrence KC MP for Burton 1974-97; Temple

Men in tights

Sir,

With regard to the suggestion that the King wear silk stockings for the coronation ("Don't chicken out, Charles, a king should don silk stockings for a coronation", Times2, Jan 23), when I took silk in 2008 my senior clerk came to see me, saying that he had a matter of great importance to discuss. I was expecting some secret linked to my newfound status. Instead, I was told: "Sir, you'll be wearing breeches for the ceremony. You urgently need to go and buy some tights, denier 80, before they all sell out round here."

Guy Morpuss KC Farnham, Surrey

Present arms

Sir,

I was slightly dismayed to see members of the Guards regiments carrying umbrellas at the King's coronation, until I realised that they were for the benefit of guests. The Duke of Wellington forbade the use of umbrellas during the Peninsular War. At Bayonne in December 1814, one officer was rebuked for allowing his men to carry them. The duke said: "The Guards may, in uniform, when on duty at St James', carry umbrellas if they please, but in the field it is not only ridiculous but unmilitary." Standing orders for the army thereafter said categorically that "umbrellas will not be opened in the presence of the enemy".

Professor Tim Connell Gresham College

Sir,

Professor Tim Connell (letter, May 8) observes that standing orders for the army categorically state that "umbrellas will not be opened in the presence of the enemy". However, that did not deter Major Digby Tatham-Warter in the Second World War. He could not remember passwords but knew that it would be generally recognised that "only a bloody fool of an Englishman would carry an umbrella into battle". At Arnhem (he was later immortalised by Christopher Good in the film *A Bridge Too Far*) he immobilised a German armoured car by thrusting the ferrule of his umbrella into the eye of the driver. He subsequently led the chaplain to safety, saying: "Don't worry about the bullets, I've got an umbrella." So when one sees the cavalry and guards sporting their bowler hats and umbrellas on certain occasions, it is good to know that the umbrellas are not just for show.

Dr Julian Critchlow Ditcham, Hants

Sir,

When, in 1993, I was walking with the Crown Equerry as we followed the Garter procession down the hill attired in morning dress, black top hat and rolled umbrella, it started to rain quite heavily. I asked my companion if I could open my umbrella. "No," he said, "it's part of the uniform to be kept rolled." We were both soaked.

John Briscoe Apothecary to the Royal Household at Windsor 1986-97; Woodbridge, Suffolk

Moving monarch

Sir,

Libby Purves's article "The reign of King Telly is coming to an end" (May 8) reminds me of watching the Queen's coronation in 1953 as a five-year-old. My father had nearly finished building a 12-inch telly, and all the neighbours were invited round. My main recollection was of the Queen going round and round, getting fatter then thinner as my father sat behind the telly with his screwdriver, tweaking the valves. Happy days.

Elaine Yeo Enfield, Middx

Crowned on radar

Sir,

As a nine-year-old boy in 1953 I was looking forward to the coronation of Elizabeth II (letter, May 10). However, no one in our family had a television, so one of my uncles, ex-Royal Electrical and Mechanical Engineers, scoured the local army surplus stores and bought a radar set, which he converted to receive TV pictures. On the day all the family watched the coronation live on a round 9-in screen with an eerie green glow. It was magic. Later we were able to watch the whole thing in glorious colour at the cinema but I will always remember that green glow.

John Deards Warminster, Wilts

House
and
home

Teenage swap shop

Sir,

Janice Turner (Notebook, May 6) is on to something with her idea of swapping the family young. However, I would start much earlier than their twenties: I would suggest that teenagers stay with another family for about three weeks, the time it will take for the typical teenage attitudes to set in, then they move to another host family to start the process again. This might improve the usual teenage attitude, which is consistent with studying for a GCSE in Grunt.

Katharine Minchin Easebourne, W Sussex

Drilling down

Sir,

I recently purchased a cordless power drill produced by a leading German manufacturer. It was accompanied by a manual of 216 pages, of which 12 were in English (including diagrams), a manual for the battery charger of 96 pages, seven of which were in English, and a manual for the battery of 164 pages, of which five were in English. In summary, 24 out of the 476 pages were of value and the rest constituted waste. We hear much about the need for a circular economy but surely this requires an underlying assumption that material is used before it is recycled.

Tim Cooper Emeritus professor of sustainable design and consumption, Nottingham Trent University

Switch to manual

Sir,
Tim Cooper was lucky to find 12 out of 216 pages of the instruction manual for his drill in English. We recently hired a Toyota car while on holiday. The entire manual was in what we assumed was Japanese, as was the greeting whenever we turned the car on. The garage had left the car for us at our accommodation and we had to ring them to find out how to start it.

Annie Tavener Brettenham, Suffolk

In a flutter

Sir,
Holes in expensive sweaters are distressing (letters, May 16–18), but of more than 2,500 species of beautiful British moths, only the larvae of two or three kinds cause this. Swatting or spraying moths in general is a pity. Better to get a garden moth trap and rejoice in the exquisite jewel box it will display every summer morning, thereby putting a bit of damaged cashmere into perspective.

Jennifer Galton-Fenzi Littlehempston, Devon

Sir,
Since the ban on naphthalene in mothballs and having had limited success with cedar balls, I use bars of soap in our wardrobes and sweater cupboards. Our preferred brand is Pears, one bar on each shelf, rotated for use when required in bathrooms. The soap seems to stops the moths in their tracks: I haven't had any holey garments in

years, and the wardrobes are beautifully fragranced. The disadvantage is that I have no idea where the moths go.

Lynda Gilbey Clyffe Pypard, Wilts

Sir,
After reading about the prevention of moths I'd like to share my remedy. I place an open bottle of Olbas oil and an open jar of Vicks in the corner of my sweater drawer. To date, I am moth-free.

Sandra Russell Chester

Ultra clean moths

Sir,
My late mother clearly believed that soap deterred moths. When we cleared her wardrobe and chests of drawers we found neither moths nor moth damage. We did find plenty of soap, though: the record was 42 bars in one drawer.

Tim Goldsack Newbury, Berks

Put out to grass

Sir,
Plastic lawns are indeed ecological disasters (leading article, May 14). We are lucky that our lawn is a remnant of old, species-rich meadow; we maintain it by mowing small areas, leaving the majority to flower and set seed, then cutting these "hay patches" once in autumn when the birds and voles have eaten all the seeds. It gives us immense pleasure to see the butterflies, bees and many other insects it attracts. Anyone with a little space can

create a wildlife-friendly lawn by planting native grasses and flowers; far better that than smothering the ground in plastic or concrete.

Michael Boxall Hepple, Northumberland

Statuesque beauties

Sir,
Emma Duncan (Notebook, Jul 25) is right: the hollyhock is a superb, unsurpassable plant, rising majestically from humble beginnings to share our summer enjoyment. In recent years I have spread hollyhocks from Sussex to Northumberland by giving out packets of homegrown seeds on visits, at parties and as Christmas presents, and have rejoiced in the results. Indeed, when once I bragged about the height of my finest specimens, I received competitive rejoinders from as far away as Africa.

Jeremy Lewis Hailey, Oxon

All over the map

Sir,
I share the enthusiasm of Greg Jones for "what3words" (letter, Aug 11) but would caution that enunciation is all important. Were I to have a heart attack in my home village at location "lawn.breezes.wobbling" and this were misheard by the 999 operator as "lawn.freezers.wobbling", my apparent location would be the frozen wastes of Alaska. I dread to think what the response time might be.

Dr Peter Cowling Laughton, Lincs

Flow of ideas

Sir,
My husband and I are trying to save energy wherever we can. Yesterday morning we timed each other in our separate showers: three minutes to the second. The obvious flaw here is the word "separate" but I'm afraid the days of shared ablutions, even if it means saving on water and electricity, are very much in the past. My shower is my place to ponder, even if it is limited to three minutes.

Deanne Clay Shipston-on-Stour, Warks

Silence is golden

Sir,
Robert Crampton's advice (Times2, Aug 30) on what a man should never say to a woman whisked me back to my youth in the 1960s. I was in the kitchen, sporting a new minidress and Mary Quant-style make-up, awaiting my lift, when my father walked in and asked: "Isn't it about time you were getting ready for your night out?"

Janet Cowie Shandon, Argyll & Bute

Say that again?

Sir,
Further to Janet Cowie's letter on what not to say to a woman (Sep 1; Times2, Aug 30), I can go one better. Some years ago I was still in my dressing gown when my husband said: "Are you ready to go then?"

Marion Offenbach Bushey Heath, Herts

Sir,
Standing at the top of the stairs, having changed for a company dinner, I asked my husband: "Do you think I look fat in this?" To which he replied: "No, sturdy." It was a very quiet evening.

Sheila Muir Holcombe Rogus, Somerset

Spot the difference

Sir,
I was intrigued to read your article on developments in facial recognition software ("Using your face as a password is easy as abc123", Sep 13). Our twins each have facial recognition on their new iPhones. They have discovered that although one twin can unlock both phones, her sister can unlock only her own. Clearly one is more identical than the other.

Anne Moriaty Chelmsford, Essex

Facing the truth

Sir,
Further to Anne Moriaty's letter ("Spot the difference", Sep 16), in which she revealed that one of her twins can unlock both phones but her sister can unlock only her own, my daughter was appalled recently to discover her face unlocked my phone.

Muriel Kellett Lymington, Hants

Snuggle station

Sir,
Janice Turner ("I will defy Putin — no heating until November", Sep 29) does not need to plug anything in to stay warm at her home desk. I wear a body-shaped quilted sleeping/moving around bag. It has removable feet so you can wear boots or slippers, and long arms that cover the hands when required. Various makes are available; I treated myself to one after four days without power in Storm Eunice and will never be cold at home again.

Julia Cheeseman Whinfell, Cumbria

Sock it to them

Sir,
Janice Turner should try some heated socks (Notebook, Sep 29; letter, Sep 30). I was given a pair last Christmas by a relative living in Germany. The socks use rechargeable batteries in small side-pockets, and are wonderful. If our feet are warm, it tends to mean we are. Heated clothing should be more widely available.

Alex Scott Dedham, Essex

Sir,
I was delighted that Janice Turner is postponing heating her house until November 1: All Saints' Day. My late father-in-law would heat his home from the feast of St Simon and St Jude, October 28, until the feast of St Philip and St James, May 1. Let our battle of not heating for Ukraine commence.

Peter Davies West Kirby, Wirral

Blow drying

Sir,

Like Janice Turner (Notebook, Oct 20), I loathe hotel rooms where the windows do not open. I sleep well only with some fresh air in the room, whatever the season or weather. Air conditioning is not the same, and I wake up feeling desiccated. Can I add another pet peeve about hotel rooms? Those that have a hair dryer, but in which mirrors are too far from plug sockets to be usable. This makes me disproportionately furious.

Melanie Lloyd Swansea

What a shower

Sir,

I always assume that a man has designed my hotel room (Janice Turner, Notebook, Oct 20 and letters, Oct 21) when the shower has a fixed head that cannot be lowered. Many men may like to soak their hair every day — very few women do, and the functional shower cap has yet to be invented.

Stephanie Sadler Fleet, Hants

Designer irritants

Sir,

The clue to a man having designed a hotel bathroom (letters, Oct 21-22) is when there are only three ceiling spotlights, and two are in the shower cubicle and the third is over the lavatory bowl. No need to light the make-up mirror after all.

Katharine Long Sevenoaks, Kent

Sir,
My pet peeve is one chair per hotel double room. I can't tell you how many times my husband and I have flipped a coin to see who gets the chair and who has to sit on the bed.

Geraldine Blake Worthing, W Sussex

Hotel frustration

Sir,
Katharine Long (letter, Oct 25) is right to bemoan the lack of lighting for make-up mirrors in hotel bathrooms. If you are lucky enough to have a light the next problem is that the mirror is set at a man's height — all I can see is the top of my head.

Nicky Gill Richmond, Surrey

Sir,
I always assume a man has put up the hot-air hand dryer in the ladies' lavatories. Why else would it be 2ft higher than it should be, so that the water on your wet hands runs down to your elbows, soaking your jacket?

The Venerable Christine Froude Bristol

Room for doubt

Sir,
Further to Melanie Lloyd's pet peeve with hotel hairdryers and mirrors (letter, Oct 21), may I add my own: hotels that have a hairdryer only in the bathroom. The machines are so feeble that they seize up in short order and are incapable of tackling my shoulder-length tresses. I have left a trail of burnt-out machines in the past and now pack my own hairdryer and mirror, but through gritted teeth at the lost space in my suitcase.

Anne Fanning Exeter

Night shift

Sir,
Three weeks ago (letter, Oct 8) I suggested that the hours of street lighting be reduced as an energy-saving measure and gave an example of my residential estate where the only beneficiaries of lighting until 2am were cats and the occasional hedgehog. Tonight I looked out of my window just after midnight to find all was in darkness. Such is the awesome power of the *Times* letters page.

Brian Parker Dartmouth, Devon

Lost and found

Sir,
I can sympathise, but also offer hope to Ann Treneman, whose belongings keep on going missing around the house (Notebook, Oct 28). This week I found my waterproof hat lying in the garden, somewhat chewed and faded and missing since the spring. The following day the lost back door key and house alarm fob turned up among my gardening gloves. I am hoping that "the hex" has finished with me for some time.

Melinda Sutherland Waltham, Lincs

Taken by a sprite

Sir,
There is a simple explanation for Ann Treneman's lost items (Notebook, Oct 28; letter, Oct 31). Whenever it happens in our household my wife, whose mother was Swedish, tells us that the *tomte* has taken it. Although this mythical creature is supposed to protect the household and its inhabitants at night, it has an annoying penchant for hiding things.

Christopher Murray Barford St Michael, Oxon

Sir,
Regarding Ann Treneman's Notebook on lost items, in our house we rely on a prayer to St Anthony, the patron saint of lost things: "Dear St Anthony, please come around: something is lost and it cannot be found." It works surprisingly often.

George Jones North Curry, Somerset

Machine menace

Sir,
I agree with Melanie Reid ("High-tech won't wash", Notebook, Nov 21): we really do need more women designers. Only a man would design the incessant beeps that come from the tumble dryer, dishwasher or washing machine at the end of their cycle, sometimes all at the same time. I look forward to increasing silence, as in these times of crisis I use them less frequently.

Sandra Noakes Chester

Kitchen nightmares

Sir,
I have had to tape over the headache-inducing LED lights on my cooker hood and the internal light in the fridge (letter, Nov 22). I've yet to work out how to deal with the unbelievably bright light in the tumble dryer, other than to cover the plastic window with cardboard. I would happily trade all the missing socks for an "off" switch.

Anne Johnston Dornoch, Sutherland

Seeing the light

Sir,
I too agree with Melanie Reid (Nov 21; letter, Nov 22), as only a man could have designed the interior of my Neff oven. The light is ludicrously positioned upside down in the top corner, wedged next to the element. Removing the glass cover is virtually impossible. Rubber

gloves, strap wrench, special Neff tool and two strapping sons-in-law were unable to budge it. It may sound trivial, but believe me, when you can't watch the progress of your Yorkshire puddings, it is critical. Not to be defeated, I finally managed to dislodge it by bashing it with a lump of wood and a hammer.

Dianne Hayes Bromham, Beds

DIY kitchen repairs

Sir,

I am very grateful to Dianne Hayes (letter, Nov 23). I too have a Neff oven with a light cover that up till now has been impossible to remove. She used a lump of wood and a hammer. Having now seen the light, I removed the cover by bashing it with my spurtle.

Annie McEnery Ennis, Co Clare

Separate snuggling

Sir,

I agree with Alice-Azania Jarvis about single duvets (Times2, Nov 23). I lived in Scandinavia for 26 years and never used a "double" duvet and knew nobody who did. Apart from the obvious temperature benefits of single duvets (summer/winter, male/female) there is another advantage: changing the covers is so much easier.

John Stephenson Middleton Cheney, Oxon

Wheel deal

Sir,
Further to Hilary Rose's Notebook (Dec 8), cars are not designed to go wrong in the first year so that the warranty will cover the fault. Instead they are designed to go wrong at the start of year four, after the three-year warranty has expired.

Joanne Aston Thirsk, N Yorks

Art of the deal

Sir,
Fitted kitchen salesmen make speculative calls similar to those of double-glazing companies (letters, Dec 30 and Dec 31). We live in a Grade II* listed house dating from the early 1300s and I had a call from an enthusiastic salesman whose opening gambit was, "How old are your kitchen units?" I looked at our Welsh oak deuddarn and tridarn and replied "1739 and 1696". There was a long pause before the irrepressible young man announced triumphantly, "Well, time to get new ones!".

Caroline Dyer Burwell, Cambs

Order of the bath

Sir,
It is always a great pleasure to immerse myself in my wife's nightly bedtime bathwater after she has vacated the bath (Janice Turner, Notebook, Jan 12). As the First World War song goes: "Wash me in the water that you

washed your dirty daughter in, and I shall be whiter than the whitewash on the wall." It is a guaranteed way to enjoy a good night's sleep.

Jonathan Frappell Yelverton, Devon

Single beds

Sir,
When we went shopping for a larger single bed like the one that Ann Treneman saw at Charleston farmhouse (Notebook, Jan 13), the salesman did not call it a "three quarter" but, with a slight glint in his eye, an "occasional two".

Jeff Cornacchia Henley-on-Thames, Oxon

Sir,
At Heal's years ago I was told that 3ft 6in-wide beds were called "wide singles" and those that were 4ft 6in "narrow doubles". When I asked for the name of 4ft-wide beds, the immediate response was: "Gentlemen's occasionals, sir."

Christopher Dean Oakington, Cambs

Sir,
I was always led to believe that a 4ft-wide bed was called a "bachelor's double".

Michael Buckley Petersfield, Hants

Pantry in motion

Sir,

I challenge Ann Treneman's assertion that pantries are almost a thing of the past (Notebook, Jan 21). As an architect who remodels domestic properties, I am increasingly being asked to include a pantry. Many houses lost their pantries with the advent of the fitted kitchen in the 1980s. With the preference now for sleek, open-plan kitchen/living spaces, pantries provide the opportunity to hide away the clutter while keeping it handy. Perhaps the need to save energy will also provide further encouragement for the natural fridge effect of the traditional pantry?

Anne Owen Twyford, Berks

Sir,

Anne Owen (letter, Jan 24) is spot on. My Edwardian home has a proper pantry, a room about 12ft by 4ft, off the north side of the kitchen, and so beautifully cool all year round. My house was valued last year and the rather excited agent said I should expect to be offered the asking price in days. When I asked why she was so confident, she replied: "The pantry."

Camay Chapman-Cameron March, Cambs

Sir,

I am confused by Ann Treneman's Notebook (Jan 21; letters, Jan 24 & 25). Surely the small cold room for keeping food fresh was always the larder. The pantry was for the pans and there was always a large sink for washing them. The silver would also be cleaned in the pantry. The scullery was for cleaning shoes and boots and feeding the dogs. Our 1937 flats had a larder in the original plans, as did the houses I knew as a child.

Amanda Tempest-Radford Norwich

Sir,
Our pantry was also on the north side of the house (letter, Jan 25). In our seven years there without a fridge, no perishable foodstuffs ever went off; likewise the milk, which stood in a bucket of water. Happy times.

Gill Moss Poulton-le-Fylde, Lancs

Sir,
At my Cambridge college we had a pantry and a buttery. I was told that the Normans had introduced these words, which had nothing to do with pans or butter (Notebook, Jan 21; letters, Jan 25 & 26). They had originally been where you kept *pain* and *bouteilles*. A larder, surely, would have been for keeping bacon.

Dr Martin Press Southampton

Sir,
I have a very personal reason to support the pantry. During the Second World War my mother laid me under the shelf in ours when the Germans bombed Sheffield.

Ken Brotherhood Heaton Mersey, Stockport

Sir,
Ken Brotherhood's letter about the pantry (Jan 27) brought back memories. As a child in 1939 I was intrigued when my father brought home a large, sturdy cardboard box and put it in the pantry. He said that it was

the "invasion box" and we were going to fill it with non-perishable food so that we would have something to eat when the Germans invaded. I still remember the secure feeling that my dad had got the Germans sorted. Once full, it stayed there until 1945 when, still on rations, we enjoyed some tasty meals as my mother cooked the contents.

Margaret Marriott Sheffield

Theft-proof bike

Sir,
Further to Tom Whipple's article "I have owned 11 bikes. This is how they were all stolen", Times2, Jan 25, my father had a solution to this problem. He painted the whole of his bicycle — frame, wheel rims, spokes, handlebars, stems and mudguards etc — a vile shade of brown. It never was stolen, and after he died I sadly had to take it to the council dump.

Eric Roberts Farnham, Surrey

Garden gym

Sir,
I am filled with abject horror that, a decade from now, a robot could attend to 40 per cent of my gardening activities ("Put your feet up, the chorebots are coming", Feb 23). I would have to join a gym.

Callum Beaton St Martin's, Guernsey

Bloated utensils

Sir,

Clare Eggington (letter, Mar 10) is right about the huge increase in portion sizes over the past 30 years, but is this because we have become more greedy or because we think we have to fill a larger plate? The handed-down draining spoon, ladle, serving spoon and slotted turner that faithfully graced my mother-in-law's kitchen since the 1970s look like children's toys, dwarfed as they are by their modern-day replacements, which are super-sized to cater for our apparent requirements. The only items from that era that remain the same size are egg cups.

William Casement Benenden, Kent

Grateful guests

Sir,

My favourite guests don't just strip their beds the morning afterwards ("Bring a bottle … of shampoo", Carol Midgley, Times2, Mar 8) but load the bedding into the washing machine too.

Jackie Wilson Llandevaud, Gwent

Stand by your beds

Sir,

At the end of our summer holiday our housesitters didn't just load their bedding into the washing machine (letter, Mar 9) but washed their sheets and pillowcases, ironed them and made up the bed for our next visitors.

Anthony Palmer Harting, W Sussex

Sir,
Jackie Wilson's guests would be jumping the gun here in Jersey. Owing to the vagaries of the weather and its effect on transport off the island, beds are never stripped until we are sure that the flight or ship has departed.

Meriel Edwards St Brelade, Jersey

Sir,
Meriel Edwards sensibly waits until her guests' flight or ship has departed before stripping the bed. I hope she waits until they have landed or disembarked before putting on the washing machine: one of my mother's many inexplicable superstitions is that it is unlucky to do laundry when someone you love is travelling.

Charlie Rapple Oxford

Waste not, want not

Sir,
Janice Turner is correct about equipment wastage (Notebook, Mar 23). I took great delight in repairing my wife's 45-year-old Kenwood Mixer. A YouTube video showed me how to disassemble it and an internet search allowed me to find the replacement parts, delivered to my home. Result: a fully functioning beautifully manufactured device, ready for another 45 years of service.

Dr Nigel Barrett London SW17

Timewarp utensils

Sir,
My father was a highly skilled mechanical engineer who for years maintained and recycled every device in our home, including toasters, mixers, cars and garden machinery, and was very proud of his thrift. My mother saw this dexterity in a slightly different light, as the only wife in the street throughout the 1970s and 1980s with a top-loading washing machine, a 1920s vacuum cleaner and a range of first-generation kitchen appliances.

Mark Banham Beechingstoke, Wilts

Star exhibit

Sir,
I empathise with Mark Banham's mother ("Timewarp utensils", Mar 27). When a Hoover repair man came to fix my late mother's upright Hoover, he asked if he could instead provide her with a new one because hers was "exactly the model we've been looking for to put in our Hoover museum". We children were mortified.

Alison Hipwell Rustington, W Sussex

State of repair

Sir,
Never mind the relative age of these Hoovers (letters, Mar 28–30), I'd just like to know how their owners found a repair man.

Pamela Stockwell South Croydon

It's in the bag

Sir,
A friend who emigrated to Australia in the Sixties took her mother's ancient Hoover with her (letters, Mar 28–31). When I asked if it was still working, she said yes but she'd found a better use for it: to store her jewellery in the bag and fool burglars.

Ann Findjan Farnham, Surrey

Faithful appliances

Sir,
Jenni Russell's article about our throwaway society takes me back to the days of the VHS recorder. Mine was playing up so I took it to the local shop and spoke to the repairman. "You've had this quite a while," he said, adding: "But of course, you live on your own." I gave him a quizzical nod. "I have observed," he said, "that any mechanical or electrical equipment, from a VHS recorder to a washing machine, vacuum cleaner or car,

will last at least twice as long before a problem arises if it is operated by the same person." It is not that the one person gets used to the machine, but that the machine gets used to its handler.

Huw Beynon Llandeilo, Carmarthenshire

Old faithful

Sir,
Further to Huw Beynon's letter (Apr 20), I was never allowed to wind the clocks in our house as my father insisted that they knew who was winding them and kept better time if it was the same person each time. Each hour was a cacophony of chimes as each one kept perfect time. Alas, on my father's demise the clocks definitely do not like my hand.

Eva Gordon-Creed Norwich

Secret signals

Sir,
With regard to Esther Walker's account of being kicked under the table by her husband, who was coping with a bore ("Married couples have secret signals. Here's ours", May 11), I made a disastrous mistake and bought a glass dining table. Turns out that even if you are chewing and/or talking, you can still see what is going on under the plates.

Jane Stanford London SW13

Table footsie

Sir,
Jane Stanford says she made a "disastrous mistake" when she bought a glass dining table ("Secret signals", letter, May 12). The solution is simple and inexpensive: she need only buy a tablecloth.

John McGuinness Tyn-y-Groes, Conwy

Country
ways

Spadge of honour

Sir,

In his enjoyable Nature Notes column (Apr 28) Jonathan Tulloch refers to a house sparrow as a "spuggie" that raised the spirits of passengers waiting for a train to Redcar. As a child in Great Crosby, then in Lancashire, I knew house sparrows as "spadges".

Philip Roberts West Lulworth, Dorset

Sir,

In Scotland, or west central Scotland at least, sparrows were known as speugs ("spee ugs"). I can also recommend Duncan Macrae's version of *The Wee Cock Sparra*.

John Arthur Glasgow

Sir,

We always referred to sparrows as spyugs. Other names commonly used by us when children were stuckies for starlings, peezies for peewits, craws for rooks and jennies for wrens.

Alan G Shearer Glasgow

Sir,

In the West of Scotland in my youth, the following ditty was recited: "Twa birdies sat on a barra:/ One was a speug, the other a sparra." I can't vouch for the spelling as I have never seen it written down.

Margaret LB Anderson Canterbury

Bilberry thrill

Sir,

I cannot share Miriam Darlington's optimism of harvesting bilberries "in their thousands", even with a special comb (Nature Notes, Apr 30). I found out the hard way that bilberry picking is not for the faint-hearted: these shrubs can be deceptively bare in high season and an hour's picking yields only a fistful of berries. Apples help to eke them out in pies. In America bilberries are called huckleberries, also slang for a person of no consequence; Twain named his famous protagonist after it and it has since become a byword for self-reliance and individualism there. The traditional day to start picking bilberries in Yorkshire is the last Sunday in July, coinciding with the Gaelic festival of Lughnasadh, which marks the start of the harvest season.

Anushua Biswas Skipton, N Yorks

Sir,

Anushua Biswas's letter (May 3) brought a smile of reminiscence. When we were young my sister and I spent many happy hours on the Black Mountains, supposedly helping our parents to pick bilberries but also building dens in the bracken and playing hide and seek. One day they were surprised at the large quantity of berries we had amassed and congratulated us. On getting home my mother was dismayed to find that most of my sister's haul consisted of sheep droppings. An easy mistake to make when you are four — or perhaps it's an early sign of a creative mind.

Jacqui Warren Abergavenny, Monmouthshire

Got your number

Sir,
Charlie Flindt rightly says (letter, May 7) that the numberplate collects more splats than the windscreen. When I stayed in digs in Andover some years ago, breakfast with the latest overnight visitors invariably included a straight-faced observation from my host that it was the practice of Hampshire police to stop motorists and measure the width of the splats on the front numberplate. From this they could calculate the vehicle's speed and would impose a heavy fine for anything over 90 mph. As I left for work I very often drove past last night's gullible visitors, scrubbing their numberplates before setting off.

Dan Lyon Lytham St Annes, Lancs

Sir,
In the 1950s my mother-in-law reluctantly lent me her Sunbeam Talbot so that my future wife and I could visit friends in the country. Her only condition was that I was not to exceed 60 mph. When I returned the car her first words were: "You didn't keep your word." I asked for an explanation. She pointed at the windscreen, on which there were a lot of squashed flies, and said that only happened when the speed exceeded 60 mph. For once I was lost for words.

Phillip Sober London W8

Soaked oak

Sir,

I was interested in your article "Oak table was 5,000 years in the making", May 11. My family business, Kerridges of Cambridge, developed a way of preserving bog oaks by steam drying in the 1970s and made a number of items, including a Welsh dresser for my father Kelsey Kerridge, which we still have in the family. However, it was believed that these oaks dated back much further, circa 75,000 years ago. We also made a pair of doors from bog oak and modern oak for Melbourne University, as my parents were good friends of the Newton-John family; Bryn Newton-John was master of Ormond College there, and was the father of Olivia.

Paul Kerridge Director, KJ Holdings; Barton Mills

Stable monarchy

Sir,

As an amateur walking stick maker I was very pleased to see from the photograph on your front page of the Queen at the Windsor Horse Show (May 16) that she has changed to using a thumb stick. This will give her more stability and confidence and help her posture more than using the seemingly ever-popular and shorter "granny" stick, which gives very little support at all.

Tim Jay President emeritus, Royal College of Chiropractors; Taunton, Somerset

Serpentine stick

Sir,
On Royal Deeside the thumbstick is better known as a snake-stick, it being carefully dimensioned, when inverted, to fit round the neck of an adder should one be encountered in the hills and moors of the eastern Cairngorms, as well as giving extra purchase on the steeper ground.

Roger Lindsay East Horsley, Surrey

Thumbs up

Sir,
Having been treated by Tim Jay (letters, May 17 & 18) I can attest to his expertise as a chiropractor, but as a stick maker he omitted a vital fact about the thumb-stick: its many uses other than as a walking aid. I acquired one recently and my wife immediately requisitioned it to reach the bird feeders high up on a lamp post. Years ago, before the advent of remote controls, my father used his thumbstick to change channels on the telly.

Fred A'Court Creech St Michael, Somerset

Watch the birdie

Sir,
The foxes might well be the reason for the golf balls found in Giles Coren's garden (Notebook, Jun 21) but in Caversham it is the red kites.

Anne Smith Caversham, Reading

Shivery snack

Sir,

Hilary Rose's American friend was appalled by the idea of cold beaches while she rather enjoyed them ("Watch out for the wee police! And other beach etiquette nightmares", Times2, Jun 22). In Scotland it was standard practice to go armed with what was known as a "chittery bite": a biscuit to give to your children when they came out of the sea to stop their teeth chattering from the cold.

Ian Templeton Tenterden, Kent

Missing pieces

Sir,

I am doing a jigsaw of a map of the universe. It is the most difficult jigsaw I have done. The last thing I need is the manufacturers sending me a few extra pieces because the James Webb Space Telescope has found previously undiscovered areas.

Ian Birch Northolt, Middx

Feather report

Sir,

We too have had a crushing disappointment with our owl box (Matthew Parris, Notebook, Aug 3). It was designed in great detail, hoisted up on specially built scaffolding into the sycamore tree, even furnished with luxury bedding in the shape of wood shavings. We patiently waited for the barn owl (which we regularly spot flying through the field) to adopt it. Alas, a squirrel family quickly moved in and are happily producing lots of offspring.

Serena Riley Angram, N Yorks

Late-arriving owls

Sir,
Matthew Parris (Aug 3; letter, Aug 5) needs to be patient. Our barn owl box, erected in a poplar by a (barefoot) representative from the Barn Owl Trust on a frosty morning ten years ago, became home to generations of quarrelsome wood pigeons. Until this year, that is. The sight of four owlets jostling for position on the ledge at dusk while their parents hunt silently over the field below has been a delight these past weeks, and all the more thrilling for being so unexpected.

Dermot Woolgar Sissinghurst, Kent

Sir,
We found the solution was to add a second barn owl box. Eggs are laid in one and the female can then escape her hungry chicks to have "time out" with the male in the other. A four-year vacancy was rewarded immediately.

Edward Moss London SW12

Strings attached

Sir,

Locating a hornets' nest by fitting a transmitter to a captured hornet and then releasing it is not that clever ("He's wearing a wire! Sting reveals hornet hideaway", Aug 6). As children in the 1950s we often located wasps' nests by holding a wasp gently against the window, tying a piece of cotton around its neck, and then — provided it still had its head — following it as it flew back to its nest. Your report says that using the transmitter reveals the nest's location within 40 minutes. Our method took about 30 seconds.

Leigh Belcham Warwick

Blue is the colour

Sir,

Paul Simons gives a nice mnemonic for the colours of the rainbow (Weather Eye, Aug 24). However, my favourite is Real Old Yokels Guzzle Beer In Volumes.

George Hart Rickmansworth, Herts

Sir,

I'd never heard the mnemonic for the colours of the rainbow quoted in Weather Eye but a favourite in my undergraduate days was Virgins In Bed Give You Odd Reactions.

Elizabeth Longrigg Oxford

Sir,
Elizabeth Longrigg's memory may be deficient (letter, Aug 25). My recollection of the mnemonic for the colours of the rainbow is Virgins in Bed Give You Outrageous Reactions.

William Fairney Hawkesbury Upton, Glos

Sir,
The mnemonic I was taught for colours of the rainbow at an all-girls school with a brewery foundation was Rare Old Yokels Gorge Beer in Vats.

Vanessa Nottage Hertford

Shot full of lead

Sir,
Professor Rhys Green ("Warning over eating pheasant shot with lead", Aug 23) needs to relax. I am in perfect health at 79 despite carrying in my appendix what x-rays show is about an ounce of lead ingested over 50 years of shooting and eating game birds. Over the years radiologists have panicked about intestinal cancer but we all have a laugh when I reveal the truth.

John Murray Compton Chamberlayne, Wilts

Uncommon finch

Sir,

John Lewis-Stempel says that the only chaffinch-themed verse he has encountered is Richard Jefferies' *My Chaffinch* (Nature Notebook, Sep 17). In 1965 the Scottish poet Edwin Morgan wrote the poem *Chaffinch Map of Scotland*. Morgan, Scotland's first national poet, presented this poem in print as a cleverly multi-layered picture of a chaffinch in the shape of Scotland itself.

Martin French Cumnor, Oxon

Essence of England

Sir,

While Richard Jefferies' *My Chaffinch* may well be the only entirely chaffinch-themed verse that John Lewis-Stempel has encountered (Notebook, Sep 17; letter, Sep 20), in Robert Browning's matchless *HomeThoughts from Abroad*, it is the chaffinch that so memorably "sings on the orchard bough/ In England — now!" Only a line, but what a line.

Emily Fergus London SW10

Practical plant

Sir,
John Lewis-Stempel (Nature notebook, Sep 17) notes that the yellow-flowered great mullein (*Verbascum thapsus*) is known as "donkey's ears" locally, owing to the soft fur of its leaves. In America, some instead refer to it as "camper's friend", as it is a particularly plush substitute for those caught off guard without lavatory paper in the great outdoors.

Professor Jennifer Rohn Gravesend, Kent

Genuine bog paper

Sir,
Professor Jennifer Rohn says that the leaves of the yellow-flowered great mullein make good outdoor lavatory paper (letter, Sep 19). May I point out that the best countryside tissue is damp sphagnum moss.

Andrew McLeish Bathgate, W Lothian

Listening fish

Sir,
You report (Oct 13) that Dr Adelaide Sibeaux of Oxford University has found that fish can navigate using memory. If Dr Sibeaux cares to visit my garden, she will learn that they can do a lot more than that. The fish in my pond spend most of their days hidden beneath the oxygenating plants. However, at any time between 9am and 5pm in summer I call out "Brunch, boys and girls,"

and they come swarming to whichever corner of the pond I am at, clamouring for food; which they duly get. Many friends have witnessed this, but only my voice, which, clearly, they have come to recognise, will do the trick.

Jeremy Hornsby London N1

Nutty solution

Sir,
Melissa Harrison (Nature Notes, Oct 22) is to be applauded for trying to limit the spread of Himalayan balsam, only she should not burn the seeds but eat them. Raw or roasted, they have a wonderful nutty flavour.

Michael Johnson Clevelode, Worcestershire

Feline groovy

Sir,
You report that cats are more responsive if spoken to in a silly voice ("Baby voice helps the cat get your tongue", Oct 25). I beg to differ. With my two, whether they respond depends entirely on the value of the words from the cat's point of view, "Tuna for dinner?" or "Walk round the block?" being virtually certain to elicit a favourable response whatever tone is used, in contrast to "Flea treatment today?" or "Shall we go to see the vet?", which invariably results in a speedy exit by the relevant cat through the nearest door.

Deborah Rubli Chichester

Fans on the wing

Sir,

Jonathan Tulloch (Nature Notes, Oct 26) wonders where all the starlings in London have gone. If he cares to visit Craven Cottage at dusk he will see hundreds of the birds roosting on Fulham Football Club's floodlights.

Katie Stockton London SW6

What a mess

Sir,

"Splooting" has been in our household vocabulary for years ("Vibe shift to permacrisis that defines our year in words, Nov 1). It has nothing to do with dogs cooling themselves in hot weather though. Its obvious (to me) meaning is when a quantity of mixture of, say, cake ingredients or scrambled eggs flies outside the bowl and goes splooting where it shouldn't.

Gill Moss Poulton-le-Fylde, Lancs

Sir,

Rain has been "splooting" on my car windscreen for decades (letter, Nov 2; report, Nov 1). I always assumed it was a good Scots word.

Morag Ross Knaresborough, N Yorks

Sir,
On the subject of "splooting", an alternative spelling is "spleuter", a word commonly used in Scotland (see the *Dictionaries of the Scots Language*) to mean to fall flat into liquid or mud. It can also refer to any mess.

Jim Grant London SE22

Sir,
Fifty years ago "splooting" was invented by our children to describe squeezing a boiled onion to eject the inner layers. It persists to this day.

Seymour Redstone London SW15

Poppies à la mode

Sir,
In recent years I have noticed a trend to decorate war memorials and their environs with knitted or crocheted poppies. In my own town the war memorial, gardens, hedges and railings are festooned with these creations. Our town hall and our largest hotel are similarly adorned; even the postbox has the knitted head of a combat soldier. While appreciating the skill and good intent of their creators I suspect we have reached peak knitted poppy. The effect of the preponderance of red is more of a festive feel, with its attendant jollity rather than the atmosphere of sombre reflection we should be aiming for.

Marie-Claire Dibbern Kelso, Scottish Borders

Another country

Sir,
Further to Matthew Parris's comment regarding the changing use of the word "country" (Notebook, Nov 16), you will still hear people here in Cornwall saying they are "going up country to England". Crossing the Tamar is a serious business.

Maggie Fraser Penpillick, Cornwall

Sir,
Matthew Parris may be unaware of other references to distant counties of Britain. I have been a part-time resident of the Isle of Wight for more than 20 years now, and mainland Britain is invariably referred to by the natives (Caulkheads) as "the North Island". It seems to me that this appellation keeps the larger body of land firmly in its place.

Alan Titchmarsh Cowes, Isle of Wight

Calling at Kernow

Sir,
Never mind crossing the Tamar being "a serious business" (letters, Nov 17 & 18). When I lived in Cornwall I would stand on the up country platform at Redruth station and read the doom-laden sign under the bridge: "To Truro and beyond."

Catherine Craig Harvington, Worcs

Sir,
When I became chair of the Eden Project in 2013 I addressed the staff and promised to bring more tourists

to Eden; a hand went up and I was asked if I was going to bring more of them from up north. "Do you mean from Yorkshire, where I am from?" I asked. "No," came the reply, "from Newquay."

Judith Donovan Kirkby Malzeard, N Yorks

Sir,
As a fervent Cornishman may I invite my fellow Celts north of the border to adopt a version of the answer I always give when asked my nationality: "British by birth, Cornish by the grace of God."

Jonathan Ball Co-founder, the Eden Project

No bee is an island

Sir,
Your report reveals a company that is naive in the extreme ("Our artificial honey is the bee's knees, say scientists", Nov 26; letter, Nov 29). With apology to John Donne: any bee's death diminishes me because I am involved in life. The purpose of a bee is to recycle atoms and promote the survival of hundreds of species of micro-organisms, plants and animals, including humans. Bees teach us that a society must regulate its population in relation to its economic resources. When bees in a colony run out of food, they share what is left and die together. They have done this for 30 million years. We are only herding animals aspiring to become social.

Robert Pickard Emeritus professor of neurobiology, Cardiff University

As the crow flies

Sir,
Jonathan Tulloch poses the question: "How do you tell the difference between crows and rooks?", Nature notes, Nov 30. My father, a lifelong countryman, had a simple answer. If you see a lot of crows together, they're rooks. If you see a rook by itself, it's a crow.

Stephen Bell York

Sir,
Stephen Bell's letter (Dec 2) brought back an old clerihew: "For those who really need to know, a single rook's a certain crow./ But rows of crows, despite their looks, are rooks." A handy aide-memoire.

Philip Blunden East Clandon, Surrey

Sir,
In our household we keep it simple. We call them all "crooks".

John Wheeler Hambledon, Surrey

Sir,
I'm afraid Stephen Bell's father (letter, Dec 2) was wrong in his advice to the effect that one rook is a crow. In winter corvids, particularly crows, often gather together in a "murder" and here near Archway in north London last week I saw 23 assembling for a discussion in a nearby tree.

John Batten London N6

Words of wisdom

Sir,
Max Hastings writes that "a lexicographer estimated that the average 19th-century peasant used a vocabulary of 250 words" (Notebook, Dec 28). I would query the use both of "average" and "peasant". But if I consider one of my Victorian shepherd ancestors, I agree that he would have known 250 words ... just about sheep.

Alison Brackenbury Cheltenham

Half a boy

Sir,
Madeline Macdonald (letter, Jan 24/ 2023) is right that *Lark Rise to Candleford* covers the disappearance of the days when farm labourers worked the land. I have never forgotten Flora Thompson's record of an old country saying: "One boy's a boy, two boys be half a boy, and three boys be no boy at all." In other words, the more boys that help, the less work they do.

Dr Richard Bloore Twickenham

Sir,
Dr Richard Bloore's letter (Jan 25) reminded me of a saying I saw years ago in the San Francisco Chronicle: "One boy on his own equals a brain, two boys together equals half a brain, three or more boys together equals no brains at all." I used to be deputy head at a secondary school and would use it occasionally to explain to parents why and how their sons ended up in trouble. It always worked.

Tom Clelland Lanark

Science of dowsing

Sir,

A rational explanation for the use of dowsing rods by some water company employees (report, Jan 30) is that these staff have an inherited ability to sense local variations in the Earth's magnetic field. Homing pigeons and migrating birds also utilise the magnetic field. My first experience, 40 years ago, was of using two bent metal coat hangers as rods to locate the field drains under a disused tennis court. I and my two daughters have subsequently located numerous house drains and buried water pipes, with my younger daughter identifying the electricity supply trench to their property in Spain last year.

Dr John Dawson Ret'd engineer Worsley, Greater Manchester

Sir,

Dowsing not only finds water but also metal. When the engineers at the chemical plant in Cambridgeshire where I worked as a supervisor needed to find the position of multiple underground metal pipes before excavating the ground, I suggested they lend me a couple of welding rods instead of consulting the site plans. Bent into right angles, the rods enabled me to pinpoint the hidden pipes. The engineers followed me around in amazement, marking the ground as we went. I have no idea how it works, but it does, if not for everyone.

Nigel Paine St Austell, Cornwall

Sir,
My mother was an excellent dowser (letters, Feb 1) and could find water or metals easily; she was able to pass on this skill to me for a short time if she held my hand.
The skill has been passed on to my sisters and daughters. It works.

Kenneth Williams Leominster, Herefordshire

Sir,
I find the best way to do it is to use two bent metal coat hangers with the ends placed in empty Biro tubes. These form handles and enable the metal to swivel easily.

Deborah Swaine Streat, E Sussex

In other words

Sir,
In her report "Kalsarikännit, the joy we can't translate into English", Mar 3, Lucy Bannerman includes the Italian word *friolero*, "one who is acutely sensitive to the cold". For those of us who live further north, in Sheffield, the word "nesh" is used frequently for the same reason.

Clare Beard Sheffield

Sir,
I am Welsh and although the Welsh language has many words with no English equivalent, my own favourite is the Scottish Gaelic word *Sgriob*, which means the tingle of anticipation on the upper lip before drinking whisky.

Lynda Wallace Kilmarnock, Ayrshire

Sir,

Working in northeast Namibia, I discovered Silozi, a wonderfully expressive language giving a fresh insight via its portmanteau words into the really important things in life. My absolute favourite word is *kuambelela,* meaning "to order a crocodile by witchcraft to return its victim". I'm wondering if English is a little on the wordy side.

Marian Shaw Berrick Salome, Oxon

Sir,

On untranslatable words (letters, Mar 4 & 6), many times in my life I could have used the Georgian word *shemomechama*, which means: "I am enjoying my meal so much that I accidentally ate the whole thing."

David Osmond Barnoldby le Beck, Lincs

Sir,

The Russian word *vranyo* is a very specific type of lie, meaning: "You know I'm lying, and I know that you know, but I go ahead with a straight face, and you nod seriously and take notes." The Kremlin has taken this approach over Ukraine.

Peter Butt Royal Wootton Bassett, Wilts

Stain with a nip

Sir,

Further to your report "Bees' 6ft honeycomb under floorboards of family home" (Mar 14), a few years ago in the nature conservation centre in Northern Ireland where I worked we noticed a spreading black stain on the ceiling of a corridor. My colleague rubbed his finger on it before tasting it, and unsurprisingly found that it was "unpleasant". We then removed one of the ceiling lights to have a look — and were greeted by three pine marten pups looking down on us. The black stain was emanating from their toilet corner, so I for one would not advocate tasting a damp patch in the home.

Richard Watson Enniskillen, Co Fermanagh

Bullfinch decree

Sir,
Henry VIII's act of parliament "promising a penny for every dead bullfinch" for eating fruit buds (Nature notes, Mar 16) was to include many other species. Hedgehogs, wrongly believed to suck milk from the teats of recumbent cows at night, attracted a twopence bounty: shockingly, parish records show half a million were paid in one period before abolition of the act in the 18th century.

Peter Saunders Salisbury

Bounties outfoxed

Sir,
Further to Peter Saunders's letter (Mar 17), there is a more recent example of government bounties. In Ireland in the 1970s a bounty was paid for killing foxes. In the Republic the tongue was needed as evidence; in Northern Ireland the brush. This lack of cross-border co-ordination was lucrative to fox hunters near the border.

Christopher Bellew London W6

Chasing a tail

Sir,

Further to the letters about bounties, faced with rats spreading diseases including the plague in Hanoi in the early 1900s, the French governor introduced a bounty: one cent for every rat tail presented to officials. The result was an explosion in the rat population as people bred them to earn an income.

Jeremy Ratcliffe Felixstowe, Suffolk

Shorne by sheep

Sir,

In past centuries sheep were not uncommon in churchyards, which were often managed as hay meadows: the hay would be cut in the summer, after which sheep would be used to graze the aftermath — and tread in the wildflower seeds. Many clergy kept a horse or two for visiting outlying parishioners and the hay crop went to the rector for his animals and made up part of his stipend. This right to the hay crop was protected by a statute of Edward I: if anyone should damage the rector's hay crop he could demand compensation. In the late 19th century a rector did in fact sue a woman for cutting the grass on her sister's grave, thus depriving him of some of his winter hay.

Elizabeth Hardcastle York

Sir,
When I was vicar of a small town parish with a large churchyard in Kent I had to mow the grass. A local shepherd saw me struggling and offered to bring some sheep along to help me keep the grass short around the many headstones. He also erected a fence to corral them safely. The sheep had other thoughts and several of them leapt the fence and set off down the high street, where they took refuge in the car park of the doctors' surgery. Although the sheep caused chaos, I did not blame them for choosing life over death.

Canon Brian Stevenson
West Peckham, Kent

World
of
work

Swine fever

Sir,

Libby Purves's "lived experience" of being the only English girl at her French school ("Microaggression is best seen off with scorn or a shrug", Thunderer, May 11) revived an ancient memory of my sister and me as the only two British pupils in a school near Paris, where we were assumed to be English and were called "English pigs". Setting matters right worked a treat and we were only occasionally referred to thereafter as "Scottish pigs". Vive la différence …

Gilly Hendry Gullane, East Lothian

Lure Russian exiles

Sir,

Reading David Aaronovitch's column ("Russian exiles deserve red carpet treatment", May 12) reminded me of a poster I used to have on my wall when I worked in Geneva. Below a picture of Albert Einstein it read: "A suitcase isn't the only thing a refugee brings to their new country."

Karen Butler North Luffenham, Rutland

Numbers game

Sir,

Further to your report "Give maths a less scary name, ministers told", May 17; letters, May 18, "maths" is intimidating and "numeracy" sounds boring. Years ago my daughter's school introduced a lunchtime maths club. No one turned up. The school then introduced a lunchtime puzzle club. Everyone came.

Sharon Footerman London NW4

Four-day week trial

Sir,

In the 1970s the unions representing the oil industry in Australia negotiated a four-day week for workers ("Long weekends to carry on as 70 firms trial four-day week", Jun 6). I was working there then and enjoyed the additional time off, but it came at a price. Different companies were allowed to arrange their own days off, and the result was chaotic. If I in company "A" wished to speak to a person in company "B", I might be told that person was on their day off and would call me back tomorrow. But tomorrow was my day off, and then it was the weekend. The result was that normal contact between companies became bogged down. In due course the practice was dropped and the five-day week was resumed. One hopes that if four-day weeks were introduced in the UK, the day off would be the same for everyone.

Michael Ridd Former chief geologist, BP Australia

Working weak

Sir,

Michael Ridd's experience of the four-day week in Australia (letter, Jun 7) was chaotic but when I introduced one in the 1970s at *TV Times* magazine it worked extremely well: staff worked four long days to get the magazine to press on Thursday night, which gave much more time to get it on sale on Saturday. The journalists had Friday off. Unfortunately, at the Christmas party, the editor asked the wives of the sub-editors how their husbands were enjoying the new regime. The reply was: "You are working them far too hard — they come home exhausted on Friday night." Goodness knows what they got up to.

Mike Roberts South Cheriton, Somerset

That Friday feeling

Sir,

As editorial director of *TV Times*, which conceded a four-day week in the turbulent 1970s (letter, Jun 9), I can solve the mystery of what the journalists got up to on the fifth day. As part of the union negotiations we also agreed to provide journalists with daily luncheon vouchers — surely, I thought, a shameful betrayal of Fleet Street's three-hour lunches, as these paper tokens were worth only a few shillings and were usually the preserve of junior clerical staff. But no. On Fridays a bunch of enterprising sub-editors secured an agreement that their weekly ration of four LVs would be regarded as legal tender for admission to a Soho drinking club.

Peter Jackson South Barrow, Somerset

Trial by television

Sir,

Further to your report "Television cameras to film in crown court" (Jul 28), the sentencing remarks by a judge will explain the reasons and constraints for a sentence, which may otherwise seem inadequate or excessive. The public are entitled to know, though not always with the zeal of a habitual attender in the public gallery at one of my courts, who had ten numbered cards, which he held up to show his approval or otherwise of my decisions. The sentence is the second most dramatic point, and viewers may particularly watch out for any short pause, after which the words "suspended for two years" may, or may not, follow.

His Honour Barrington Black London NW3

Wapping warrior

Sir,

Charlie Wilson (obituary, Sep 3) was the finest editor I worked for in more than a half-century in journalism. The only time he really got mad with me was when I was in the office in London pulling together a story on a ferocious hurricane that had hit the Caribbean. To amuse the sub-editors I sent across the story with the byline "By Joe Bloggs in Antigua and David Sapsted who wishes he was". Unfortunately it wasn't spotted until it appeared on page one of the first edition. The next day Charlie was furious and gave me what is best described as a colourful dressing down in the middle of the newsroom. When he had finished, I asked if he was so cross because

I should have written "who wishes he were" rather than "was". For a moment, Charlie stiffened in anger. Then he exploded in laughter, called me an extremely rude name and walked off, shaking his head and telling me I was "a hopeless case".

David Sapsted Westfield, E Sussex

Naked justice

Sir,
I agree with His Honour David Ticehurst's reasons for keeping wigs, both for advocates and judges (letter, Sep 12). Once, when moving to another court centre, I left my wig behind. It was too late to drive the round trip of 80 miles to get it so I sat wigless for the day, as did the advocates in considerate support. All was well until I had to pass a sentence of ten years. At that point the proceedings lacked the formality and solemnity that they deserved: I felt distinctly underdressed and overexposed.

His Honour Simon Tonking Paris

Clothing of justice

Sir,
David Ticehurst (Sep 12) likes the anonymity a wig gives you in court but I would describe it as an essential disguise. At Wood Green crown court I once sentenced a prolific burglar to seven years in prison. There was an immediate uproar from his many friends and supporters; his furious mother questioned my paternity in no uncertain terms. I adjourned court with as much dignity as I could muster, and

as it was my last case that day I changed and decided to go down the main staircase into the public part of the building. There the mother was still fulminating: "If I ever see that f***ing judge again, I'll murder him. And it will be a long, slow and painful death." I walked right past her and her angry friends and family. Not one of them recognised me.

His Honour Nicholas Browne Circuit judge 2006–17; London NW5

Sir,
Before discarding the court wig, critics might reflect that the Supreme Court judiciary abandoned theirs in favour of a gown, emblazoned with an insignia on the back which, for all the world, looks exactly like a target.

His Honour Peter Moss Haslemere, Surrey

Oxford excrescence

Sir,
Further to your report "Coffey vows to purge Oxford comma" (news, Sep 16), it is worrying that the health secretary appears to give priority to the abuse of a comma when hospital waiting lists are full of patients worrying about a colon.

Robert Woodcock KC Netherton, Northumberland

Sir,
The Oxford comma is not always helpful in avoiding confusion. The statement "I would like to thank my father, the Pope, and Dame Judi Dench" might give the wrong impression of my paternal parentage.

Dr Jane Skinner Cambridge

Challenge of year 9

Sir,
You report that Jonathan Gullis, the new education minister, is "a former head of year 9" ("Education role for former teacher who wants more grammars", Sep 16). Anyone who has taught in a secondary school will treasure their memories of that tough old year, squeezed between cheery new year 7s and studious year 10 and year 11 pupils, who are too busy with GCSEs to be a bother. But oh, those year 9s. Trust me, if he can handle year 9, the Department for Education will be a doddle.

Hilary Moriarty Former head teacher and CEO, the Boarding Schools' Association

Dreading Mondays

Sir,
That seven in ten people get the "Sunday Scaries" because they dread going to work on Mondays (news, Oct 10) prompts me to suggest the solution that worked for me for years. From the early 1990s until I retired in 2016 from the head office of a law firm, I met a friend for lunch on Mondays at a nearby restaurant, where we played one or more games of chess while eating. This may not have been ideal for digestion but it transformed Mondays into a day to which we looked forward. The principle could easily be applied to most people's circumstances. In essence, it involves looking on the bright side of life.

John Knott Lancing, W Sussex

Neutral separation

Sir,
My grandson tells me that at his school lavatories are already labelled "gender-neutral" ("Schools face having single-sex and gender-neutral lavatories", Nov 11). All the boys choose to go to the left and the girls choose to go to the right. Problem solved, no extra signage needed.

Ruth Snary Bristol

This spells trouble

Sir,
The English Spelling Society has failed to grasp a fundamental flaw in its plan to reform English spelling (report, Nov 23). Its system tries to represent sounds, as in wash becoming "wosh". This takes no account of regional variations in pronunciation. Love could become "luv" in lots of places, but in Huddersfield it would need to be "lov", and blue in Barnsley would not be "bloo" but "blew". I am sure the same would apply for certain words throughout the British Isles.

Peter J Robinson Wakefield, W Yorks

Sir,
The Church of England's liturgy committees, like the English Spelling Society, sometimes seem unaware of regional differences in pronunciation. The phrase "preserve our souls and bodies" sounds less than reverent when intoned by those of us who pronounce "our" as "ar".

The Rev Janet Fife Whitby, N Yorks

Terrific teacher

Sir,
Hilary Moriarty says there is no "Wow!" factor in teaching (letter, Nov 24). A few days ago I received a copy of a book by a former pupil inscribed: "Thanks for the past — it is now my future." Beat that.

Jane Whiter Old Basing, Hants

In the line of fire

Sir,
Using the armed forces to help out during strikes has a long history. In the 1977 firemen's strike, my flight sergeant was sent off to run a section of servicemen with a "Green Goddess" fire engine in a town in Wales. When I visited them I found them all wearing T-shirts proclaiming: "Join the RAF and go to blazes."

Air Commodore Iain McCoubrey Letcombe Regis, Oxon

One out, all out

Sir,
In solidarity with our ever-helpful postman we have decided that our usual Christmas card "box" to him containing a banknote, which over time has increased in denomination, will this year contain only a note saying regretfully that we are also on strike.

Pat Longuet London NW7

Harmful language

Sir,
I wish Stanford University well in its effort to eliminate harmful language from its computer code ("US college to erase phrases 'causing harm'", Dec 21). The company I worked for carried out an annual audit of all files for inappropriate language. This resulted in hundreds of references to sex. This was where one word or code ended in "s" and was followed by one starting with "ex".

Colin Macduff-Duncan Oxshott, Surrey

Sex machine

Sir,
Colin Macduff-Duncan's letter (Dec 23) reminds me of a simple personnel database my office had to manage in the 1980s. The data entry clerks found that if they forgot to enter "M" or "F" with a person's other data, the message "Sex is mandatory, please enter" would appear.

Joanne Aston Norby, N Yorks

Plane clothes

Sir,
As soon as I saw the pictures of the new BA uniform jumpsuit (news, Jan 7), I looked to see who had designed them and, yes, it was a man (Ozwald Boateng). It had to be because all women know what a problem it is to use "the facilities" when wearing a jumpsuit. Imagine having to do that in the confines of an aeroplane lavatory. Good luck to all the staff who wear these garments.

Sue West Camberley, Surrey

Early retirement

Sir,
Giles Coren ("Shut it, shirkers, retirement is deadly boring", Jan 28) complains that we early retirees fart all day. That is simply not true; I have tablets for that.

Terence Burbidge Little Gransden, Cambs

Woolly thinking

Sir,
Quentin Letts (Political Sketch, Mar 2) makes the spurious claim that geography masters in the 1970s wore a sports jacket, tieless shirt, pullover and crumpled trousers with brown shoes, in referring to an MP (Lloyd Russell-Moyle) whom he claims was dressed in said 1970s geography master gear while standing at the bar of the House. On behalf of my fellow geography masters of that era, and especially those of us lucky enough to still be around, I

find his comments most insulting, portraying us as scruffy dressers, bracketed sartorially with Jeremy Corbyn. All the geography master colleagues I ever met only dressed in that way while off-duty, standing at a public bar. I cannot speak for public school geography masters though, which is perhaps where Mr Letts saw such gear.

David Furmston Marford, Wrexham

Opposing Ofsted

Sir,
The debate about the role of Ofsted brought to mind an experience during one of the inspections I experienced in the course of my career as a head teacher. I took a dislike to the lead inspector and, unable to affect the way he and his team conducted their inquiries, I adopted a different approach. At the start of the week-long ordeal I made a small Plasticine model of him and every time I went to my office after meeting him I stuck a pin in. By the middle of the week he was complaining of back pains, which got progressively worse. On the last day he had to be helped to his car and his discomfort was plain for all to see.

Childish as it may now seem, I took comfort from this small victory and it helped me, and my staff, to cope with an otherwise unpleasant experience.

Dr Richard Greenfield Staverton, Northants

Becket aberration

Sir,
Jack Blackburn's piece on how the "à" got intruded into the name of Thomas Becket was very interesting ("Becket's troublesome preposition was a Protestant slur", Mar 25). In 1976 I was examining in the history finals at Oxford, and in the English medieval history paper a question set was: "Why did Thomas Becket choose martyrdom?" (Despite assumptions at the time, it was not in fact I who set it.) The paper left the examiners' final proofreading with "Thomas Becket" but when it came back from the printers on the morning of the exam it read "Thomas à Becket": some know-all at the printers had added the "à". As the "à" was at that time the hallmark of everyone who didn't know what they were talking about, I tried to persuade my two fellow medievalist examiners, now both sadly deceased, to sue the printing press for £20,000 for loss of professional reputation, but they were too pusillanimous to take up the cudgels.

Henry Mayr-Harting Oxford

Sir,
A further printer's biblical "sin" (TMS, Mar 29) relates to the translation of Luke 1.15 in the late-14th-century Wycliffe Bible. In the angel's prophecy to Zechariah that his son John the Baptist would be both great in the sight of the Lord and abstemious in his drinking habits, "strong drink" is translated as "sidir". A copy of what became known as the Cider Bible exists in Hereford Cathedral's chained library. The precept about temperance has not subsequently been universally followed in the West Country.

Howard Tomlinson Hereford

Future is AI

Sir,

As an academic lecturing on law and technology, I was intrigued by William Hague's analysis, in which he wisely concluded we have a lot to fear from AI ("World must wake up to speed and scale of AI", Apr 4). Coincidentally in my lectures yesterday I discussed a similar theme, concluding with my re-imagination of Martin Niemöller's famous dictum: First, they came for the data, and I did not speak out — because my data was anonymous. Then they came with facial recognition, and I did not speak out — because I was not a subject of bias. Then they came for my freedom of speech, and I did not speak out — because I was not cancelled. Then they came for my smartphone — and there was only Siri left to speak for me.

Dr David Cowan Assistant professor, School of Law and Criminology, Maynooth University

Sir,

Technocrats' decision to "pause" exploration into the possibilities of AI ("Musk: Rein in AI before it outsmarts us all", Mar 30) is probably based on the 1954 short story *The Answer* by Fredric Brown. The scientists develop a super-calculator connecting 96 billion planets. The final linking switch is thrown and the machine hums into life. The chief scientist then asks the fundamental question: "Is there a God?" The answer is immediate: "Yes, now there is a God." The scientist grasps the implications and tries to turn the machine off. A bolt of lightning burns him to a crisp and fuses the switch shut.

Margaret Brown Burslem, Stoke-on-Trent

Taking the lead

Sir,

Like Hannah Skelley ("Guess why I'm picking up other people's dog poo", Times2, Apr 5), I am a twenty-something (25, to be exact) enjoying earning some extra (pub) money by offering my services as a dog walker. Sometimes "enjoying" may be stretching it, though, and I show my inexperience, forgetting to take trainers when scheduled to walk a new dog on my way back from work, for example, which resulted in my chasing after a springer spaniel through the park in my high heels (to the considerable amusement of a group of teenage boys, who seemed not to mind the interruption to their rugby). I do automatically ensure I'm armed with poo bags now, though, even if only popping to the shops.

Maisie Davis London W3

School exchanges

Sir,

Harry Hudson is right: school trips are essential (Thunderer, Apr 6). I have spent my career working in, advising and governing state secondary schools. Five years ago at an awards evening I spoke to the student who had demonstrated the most outstanding all-round achievement. I asked her if she could tell me the three most important elements that had driven her learning at secondary school. She replied: "The exchange visit to Spain, the exchange visit to France and the exchange visit to Germany."

Andy Mortimer Keyworth, Notts

Very special editions

Sir,

£20 for a hardback (letter, Apr 5)? That's nothing.
Management for Engineers, Scientists and Technologists,
which I co-authored, costs £66. No wonder hardly
anyone buys it.

John Chelsom Beckenham, Kent

Sir,

£66 for John Chelsom's hardback book is nothing
(letters, Apr 5 & 6). The latest copy of the *White Book*,
the manual for civil litigation practice, costs £929 … a
bargain when you throw in the fact that delivery is free.

Caroline Clarke-Jervoise Barrister, London SW6

Sir,

Caroline Clarke-Jervoise (letter, Apr 8) describes the
White Book of civil litigation practice as a bargain at
£929. No such bargains are to be had at the coalface of
legal proceedings: a 500-page copy of the transcript of
a five-day trial at Winchester crown court set us back
£2,750.

Paul Turner Rudloe, Wilts

Sir,

Don't forget *Jane's Fighting Ships*, priced at £1,471
(letters, Apr 5, 6 & 8). I find our older copies very useful
to reach the top shelf, but don't tell my husband.

Ann Saunders Petersfield, Hants

Tea up

Sir,
Harry Wallop is absolutely right to sing the praises of the tea trolley (Business, Apr 14). I remember the tea breaks in my first office job: hot buttered scones and cakes baked on the premises. A pack of cards would be produced and four of us would manage a couple of rounds of Solo before the 20 minutes were up. Happy days.

Elizabeth Clarke Sheffield

Do the maths

Sir,

I agree with Sam Sims, the head of the charity National Numeracy, that addressing poor numeracy should start much earlier than 16. My daughter struggled with maths and I was castigated by her primary school for attempting to teach her long division in an understandable way, not in the cackhanded manner imposed by the school. My objection was vindicated when I found that one of my daughter's sums in her homework had been marked "wrong" when, in fact, it was correct. I wrote "See me!" in red ink in her exercise book and was duly summoned to see the headmaster for my impudence: I left with the suitably chastised headmaster sitting ruefully behind his desk.

Dr Malcolm Andrew Quorn, Leics

Medical
matters

Stone labour pains

Sir,
Janice Turner's husband (Notebook, Apr 28) might like to follow my urologist's advice who, after removing my kidney stone, suggested drinking pints of beer to avoid stones forming. When asked, "Wouldn't that be bad for my liver or heart?", he replied, straight-faced: "Not my department."

Peter Saunders Salisbury

Sir,
I've had three babies without pain relief and a kidney stone, and I'm with Janice Turner's husband on which is more painful.

Alison Ker Great Cambourne, Cambs

Pull the other one

Sir,
Sheila Hancock has a point ("Doctors don't know best, says Hancock", Jun 2). A GP told me of an elderly patient who, when told that the pain in her knee was perhaps down to old age, tartly replied that the other was the same age and it wasn't painful.

Katharine Minchin Easebourne, W Sussex

Recycled teeth

Sir,

Your report on the use of bones from the dead of Waterloo for fertiliser ("Riddle of troops who met their Waterloo", Jun 18) is indeed macabre but what about the teeth harvested from the battlefield to be made into dentures? These dentures were known as Waterloo teeth and were highly desirable, as their new owners could claim their teeth were real and not made of bone or ivory. The teeth were boiled in water before being sorted and sized for making the dentures, which could take six weeks. The practice continued until later in the century, with dental supply catalogues of the 1860s listing Waterloo teeth shipped in barrels from the American Civil War. Sets of Waterloo teeth can be seen in the British Dental Association Museum.

Dr John Goose Saffron Walden, Essex

Sir,

Teeth have not just been harvested for dentures (letter, Jun 20). The Shell House near Goodwood House has beautiful wall decorations. I asked my guide about the lovely mosaic floor, which did not seem to be made of shells. Teeth had been taken from deceased horses on the estate, sliced in half and polished, then used as tesserae for the floor. We could learn a thing or two about recycling from our Georgian predecessors.

June Keeble Storrington, W Sussex

Balance of opinion

Sir,

The research on our ability to balance on one leg (news, Jun 22) looks to be very valuable. However, I can do this significantly better on one leg than on the other. I am wondering what this says about my longevity.

Liz Westhorpe Cradoc, Breco

Sir,

Balancing on one leg can be greatly facilitated by putting your finger in the opposite ear while on one leg. We used to do this in karate warm-ups, as much of the time balance on one leg is needed. I don't know why it works, but it does.

Brian Arnopp Welwyn, Herts

Invisible patients

Sir,

Virtual patients were quite common when I worked as a GP ("Hologram patients are a cut above for medical students", Jun 28). Patients would receive a hospital appointment a few days after the actual date of the appointment, thereby making it impossible to attend. This was doubtless written off as "Appointment Given" and "Did Not Attend".

Dr Peter Barling Oswestry, Shropshire

Phantom patients

Sir,
With reference to invisible patients (letter, Jun 30), I have just received a letter giving me an appointment at the hospital with the words "Do not attend this appointment" highlighted in yellow.

Jill Alexander London SE21

A walk in the park

Sir,
Your article ("Step up heart health with a stroll after dinner", Aug 8) confirms something my grandmother already knew more than 70 years ago. Hence her oft-repeated phrase, "After dinner rest a while, after supper walk a mile". Good to know that modern research is catching up.

Shân Blythe Clevedon, Somerset

Modern medicine

Sir,
I sympathise with Hilary Rose ("What I learnt when my elderly parent went into hospital", Aug 29). While arranging my elderly mother's discharge from hospital recently to free up a much-needed bed, I was told that a completed form needed to be sent to an authorising manager by post. Why, I inquired, in this digital age did a paper form need to be sent by post? The response was: "Because our fax machine has broken."

Andrew Curl Standford, Hants

Onerous grades

Sir,

In relation to the A and A* A-level grades required for entry to medical schools I agree with the comment by Chris Wilson (letter, Aug 31) that "doctors do not need to be operating at genius level". This reminded me of a selection made by one of my professors when I was at university in the 1960s. His old dentist having retired, and needing to find a new dentist, he asked to see the final-year marks for dentistry. Ignoring all the top firsts he chose the student with the highest practical marks. It turned out to be an inspired choice.

Professor Robbie Burch Larne, Co Antrim

Teething problems

Sir,

As a dental student of the 1960s I would agree with Professor Robbie Burch (letter, Sep 2) that practical skills in dentists are an essential asset, but as a grounding I have always felt the three best A-levels to start would be biology, economics and English. Biology because it offers a good scientific basis, economics because as a general dental practitioner you have to run a business, and English because if your well-thought-out treatment plan fails to meet the patient's expectations the only beneficiaries of the subsequent disagreement could well be the lawyers.

Chris Gebbie Ringmer, E Sussex

Next patient

Sir,
Thérèse Coffey, the health secretary, promises to speed up doctors' appointments by using more pharmacists. Whenever I have consulted a pharmacist the advice has been to see my GP.

Kate Morris Billericay, Essex

Striking mortality

Sir,
Further to the letter (Sep 28) regarding a fall in mortality rates associated with a doctors' strike, one explanation is that the paucity of doctors in hospitals greatly reduces the ability to complete any death certificates in a timely manner.

Dr Patrick Morgan Consultant intensivist and medical examiner, Reigate, Surrey

'Sexy' menopause

Sir,
I read with interest your report "Menopause made me feel sexy, says actress", Sep 30. Sally Phillips adds: "You might feel a bit la la for a couple of years, but you get over it." It is crucial to note that the menopause is different for every woman; some do not "get over it". Menopause needs to be taken more seriously by everyone, not made light of. Phillips says she has not experienced hot flushes; on some days I can have three before 9am.

Sue Kelsall Hessle, E Yorks

Very hot flushes

Sir,

May I link two recent letters to your page, "Sexy menopause", Oct 1 and "Sock it to them", Oct 1? I am sure that many menopausal women will be familiar with the scenario: you wrap up with several layers, put your heated socks on, settle down to work/read/do housework and a hot flush hits as soon as you are warm. Within seconds, you are up, ripping those layers off, cursing those socks and gasping: "Get this off me, NOW!" It's exhausting.

Jane Woodward Sherborne, Somerset

Fishing for maggots

Sir,

Some years ago, when the supply of medical maggots (report, Nov 4) ran low and I needed some urgently for a patient, I visited a fishing tackle shop. I was told the maggots supplied for bait had stopped feeding and were hence useless for wound cleansing. Patients were very tolerant of maggots, the most unpleasant feature of their work being an irritating tickling feeling.

Dr Andrew Bamji Rye, E Sussex

Growth industry

Sir,

Your article regarding men getting their legs lengthened ("Growth industry as more men sign up to have their legs lengthened", Nov 14) reminded me of Harry Secombe, who maintained that he was taller sitting down than standing up. And indeed, when seen sitting down with others much taller than he was, this appeared to be so.

Charles Murray High Harrington, Cumbria

Surgeon's qualities

Sir,
In your obituary of Dame Clare Marx (Nov 30) I read what she had been told were the three important qualities in a surgeon. As a medical student I was vouchsafed a rather different triad. My consultant, who had a substantial private practice, told me that necessary qualities were affability, availability and ability. Two of them, he said, were important.

Michael Blinston-Jones Stelling Minnis, Kent

Smoke screen

Sir,
Dr John Lorains (letter, Jan 2) says it took a shock to stop people smoking. I was a cardiothoracic anaesthetist and every Monday morning I looked after patients having surgery for lung cancer. I lost count of the number of times the preoperative Q&A went as follows: "Do you smoke?", "No, I've given up", "When did you give up?", "Two weeks ago, when I got the diagnosis."

Jane Stanford London SW13

Special delivery

Sir,

Further to the letters on hospital births, 50 years ago, after a failed epidural because I was "anatomically peculiar", the consultant anaesthetist, from a pocket deep within his thorn-proof three-piece tweed suit, offered me snuff to "sneeze the dear child out".

Vicky Chapman Everton, Hants

Having one's cake

Sir,

If Professor Susan Jebb's exhortation not to take cakes into the office were applied to the NHS, a service already on its knees would quickly fall flat on its face. Hospital staff largely function on cake and other high-calorie comestibles that can be eaten by hand while moving between tasks. Out of idle curiosity, I once started a stopwatch after placing one of my wife's lemon drizzle cakes on the desk at the busy midwives' station — it lasted 39 seconds.

Dr David Bogod Ret'd consultant anaesthetist, West Bridgford, Notts

Medical maze

Sir,
Further to the correspondence on the training of doctors (Feb 28, Mar 2 & 3), Sir Richard Bayliss was dean of Westminster Hospital Medical School. In the 1960s he would tell the medical students that five years after qualifying they would find 50 per cent of the facts they had been taught were incorrect: the problem for the teachers was that at that precise time they did not know which 50 per cent it was. I suspect it is much the same today.

John F Colin, FRCS Ret'd consultant surgeon, Norwich

For better, for worse

Sir,
On the subject of folk remedies, three weeks before my marriage I was in close contact with children who developed measles. The incubation time would be just right to coincide with the wedding day. My Polish grandmother's advice was to hang three cloves of garlic around my neck. I wafted about in a haze of garlic "fragrance" which kept not only germs away but people too, including my fiancé. Nearly 59 years later I still have never had measles, and my husband still hates garlic.

Carol Symons London NW8

Last shall be first

Sir,
Being a pathological optimist means I think something good comes out of most things. If my name in a paper is listed alphabetically, I often come last, which in academic circles by tradition is the most senior position ("If life's unfair, blame your place in the alphabet", Apr 22). Sometimes I merit this place but not always. Alphabetism is not invariably ignominious.

John Wass Professor of endocrinology, Oxford University

Cutting remarks

Sir,
Bullying? As a junior doctor I worked for a much-loved surgeon who these days would have been accused of bullying. His outbursts were savoured by all except those in the firing line. His best, after two junior doctors had missed vital biochemical results, was: "I would like to take both of you outside and chop off your arms and legs and put you in a sack and throw you into the Thames [the hospital was near the river], and you know what? You would still be dangerous."

Jules Dussek FRCS Plaxtol, Kent

Sir,
Like Jules Dussek (letter, Apr 25) I, too, worked for a surgeon whose fuse was short and tongue acid: he was known as "the wounded buffalo". Early in my all-too-brief surgical career he tried to teach me how to remove a gall bladder. As he took over from me to stem the inevitable and torrential haemorrhage, he asked: "Where did you train? An abattoir? I wouldn't let you put down my cat." He was a brilliant surgeon, and I became a GP.

Dr Tim Howard Wimborne, Dorset

Otherwise engaged

Sir,
Retired GPs are being urged to return to work and ease the load on the NHS. I read *The Times* every day and there are many letters from colleagues whom I have met, know and have worked with. Returning to work would be difficult, as we are all rather busy at present outdoing each other by writing letters to *The Times*.

Dr David Earl ret'd GP, Brighton

Transport
of
delight

Cities of lights

Sir,
The function of Italy's traffic lights (letter, Jul 15) varies from region to region. According to one of its politicians, they are instructions in Milan, suggestions in Rome and Christmas decorations in Naples.

Paul Thomas Gowerton, Swansea

Green, amber, red

Sir,
I always thought Italian traffic lights were a unit of time, a split second being defined as the instant between the light turning green and the driver behind sounding his horn.

Charles Murray Workington, Cumbria

Sir,
Charles Murray defines an instant in time as the lapse between an Italian traffic light turning green and the driver behind sounding his horn. No longer. The *attimo nel tempo* (instant in time) has noticeably lengthened owing to the driver behind checking his smartphone.

Michael Ivy Rome

Sir,
Serving on the Nato staff in Naples 20 years ago, I was told that a red traffic light meant the bulb was working.

David Habershon Commander, Royal Navy (ret'd), Emsworth, Hants

Sir,
Green light dilemmas are not unique to Italy. In Dublin, as the lights changed, my cab driver leant out his window and asked the driver in front of him: "And what particular shade of green would you be waiting for?"

David Jeffrey West Malvern

Sir,
Years ago in the maze of one-way streets in Florence I learnt that on Italian vehicles the indicator lights show you where they have come from, not where they intend to go.

David Ticehurst Winscombe, Somerset

Ticket to freedom

Sir,
Should Lucy D'Orsi, the head of the British Transport Police, have her way and introduce monitoring of rail journeys, then it appears my wife and I will be taken in for questioning (Thunderer, Aug 4). We made the journey from Liverpool to Euston in the morning, returning to Liverpool during the afternoon. The reason for this journey? We simply enjoy train travel. We can see the views without driving, and stretch our legs if we want to. It's called freedom of choice.

David Burden Wallasey, Wirral

Many happy returns

Sir,
David Burden's letter (Aug 5) reminded me of a conversation I had with my boss when I worked for Sheffield Newspapers in the 1980s. When I said that I had been unable to contact him on the previous day, he said that he had "nipped by train, from Newark to London and back". He said that he did this several times a month, so that he could catch up on paperwork in peace, because nobody could interrupt him. Oh, the joy of life before mobile phones.

Richard Madin Buxton, Derbyshire

Underground rebel

Sir,
Jawad Iqbal (Thunderer, Aug 4; letter, Aug 5) is right to denigrate the suggestion that British Transport Police should be able to access passengers' travel data. He suggests that you might be on the Tube for six hours because you are a busker. Some years ago I spent more than 18 hours on the Underground (and have a certificate to prove it) to travel the whole circuit in one day; many still do this, though the network is considerably larger now. Should we be challenged about our motives?

George Hart Rickmansworth, Herts

Travelling light

Sir,
Those wishing to travel carrying only one piece of hand luggage (News, Aug 6) would do well to follow this advice: when going on holiday take half as many clothes as you think you need and twice as much money.

Olwen Davis Castlemorris, Pembrokeshire

Elbow protector

Sir,
Further to the letter (Aug 19) on the mandatory wearing of cycle helmets, I was puzzled on a visit to Athens in the early 1990s by the number of young motorcyclists and their pillion passengers who were riding around the city with crash helmets hooked on their elbows. My host advised me that a new law made the wearing of a helmet compulsory but had not specified where on the body it should be worn.

Professor David C Sanders Mortain, Normandy

Stately speeding

Sir,
There is a precedent for speed limits for cyclists. A family friend bid successfully for a penny farthing at a roup (auction) of a deceased elderly man's possessions in the 1960s. Among the objects that came with the bike was a notice of a fine of five shillings, dated in the 1880s, "for scorching through Newmachar on a penny farthing".

Roger Lindsay East Horsley, Surrey

E-bike speed limit

Sir,
As an e-bike fan and the owner of a derestricted one,
I read with interest your article "Amazon sells electric
bike kits to help riders break speed limits". Nov 9. My
wife is a keen cyclist and rides a normal road bike. She
rides at about 18 mph. Without derestricting my bike we
cannot cycle together, as at 16 mph it is like riding into
mud on an unrestricted e-bike. In America e-bikes are
allowed to do 20 mph; if we adopted this more sensible
speed limit it would render the whole business of
derestricting bikes unnecessary overnight.

David Hunter Colchester, Essex

Sir,
In Spain I have an e-bike restricted to 48 kph (30 mph).
This means I can circulate with the traffic rather than
holding it up. If I take the bike up to the mountain village
of Mijas I can freewheel back down to the coast at up to
72 kph (45 mph) without using any electricity. I have a
rule not to exceed my age in kilometres.

Tom Hackwood Fuengirola, Costa del Sol

Walk, don't walk

Sir,
In Newham, cyclists are allowed to ride on the pavements (letters, Mar 6). Alongside this we have the throngs of electric scooter users and people lost in their own worlds staring into their phones and hogging the pavement. As a result, I have taken to walking on the road — it's safer.

Tim Kerin London E7

Crazy golf

Sir,
Further to your report "Auf Wiedersehen to the VW Golf" (Apr 4), it has always puzzled me that the boot of a Volkswagen Golf has never been wide enough to accommodate a set of golf clubs.

Michael Mullins Perth

Cool car

Sir,
We never tried fitting golf clubs into my VW Golf (letter, Apr 6) but the feature we appreciated the most in our model was that the glovebox acted as a refrigerator. Taking our own drinks and sandwiches on long, hot summer journeys definitely helped to avoid marital disharmony caused by the stress of mobbed and expensive motorway services.

Stephen Knight Barnet, Herts

Hasta la vista, baby

Sir,
I admire Arnold Schwarzenegger's efforts in filling in a pothole (report, Apr 13), but rest assured, it will be back.

John Berry Countesthorpe, Leics

Thrill of the road

Sir,
Surely the whole point of owning a Mustang is to enjoy driving it ("Driverless Fords get the green light", Apr 14)? Watching the traffic while being driven is no fun at all; you can do that on a bus, just less comfortably.

Adrian King Bromley, Kent

Smart idea

Sir,
While driving from Cumbria to Buckinghamshire on the M6 I noticed quite long sections of the inside lane not being used by drivers ("AA condemns smart motorway 'scandal'", Apr 17). Have we created our own hard shoulder?

John Lupton Carlisle